CATCH ME WHEN I'M HAPPY

CATCH ME WHEN I'M HAPPY

Mary Jo Randle

SOUVENIR PRESS

First published 1988 by Souvenir Press Ltd,
43 Great Russell Street, London WC1B 3PA
and simultaneously in Canada
Reprinted 1989

ISBN 0 285 62867 4

Photoset, printed and bound by
Redwood Burn Limited, Trowbridge, Wiltshire

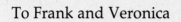
To Frank and Veronica

Facts First

NAME: Margaret Onions
STAR SIGN: Taurus
RELIGION: Left footer
FAVE COLOUR: Black
FAVE FOOD: Puddin' chips 'n' peas in a tray
FAVE SINGLE: 'Je t'aime'
LIKES: Julie Driscoll, Art College students, boutiques and
  Marsha Hunt
DISLIKES: Lorry drivers, nylons, carpet slippers, the smell
  of chewing gum, polo necks, hairy chests, beer
  bellies, bossy bus conductors, lads who spit at
  you on buses
PETS: A Swedish budgie called Inge and a mongrel dog
  called Scrap
DISTINGUISHING MARKS: None

LOCATION: A photobooth, Rochdale, Lancs., 1970

*This bird's eye view is a valuable document and should be carefully
preserved.*

7

November

Your Stars for November

The question of what you are to do with your life remains as yet unresolved. But take heart, you are not alone. Modern women everywhere are struggling with the same quandary. By nature you are a home-maker keen on guarding your little patch of peace, but this sometimes conflicts with a desire in you to go out and make your mark on the outside world. True love may be waiting for you just around the corner, but meanwhile exercise patience and you may find that has its own rewards.

Saturday, 14th November, 1970

It's Saturday night, I'm sixteen, it's chuckin' it down and I'm in on my own as per bloody usual. I have nothing, absolutely nothing to look forward to.

> Seeing them.
> Nancy and Dave.
> Dave and Nancy.
> Seeing happiness.   Nancy is beautiful
> Seeing feelings.   in mind and body.
> And feeling the sight.

I feel fat. Very fat. I ate too much cake. I've never gone out with a boy. No, really gone out with somebody. Okay, I've 'been' with lads, but I've never *really* gone out with anybody. I've never had anybody care for me, think of me, feel for me — never. I'm in need of a pedestal. Nancy's lucky, but she deserves to be lucky.

I'm miserable. Want to go to the Isle of Wight Pop Festival next year. Hope me dad'll let me go. Couldn't bear to miss it. Went to Park Cake Bakeries today for a job during Rochdale holidays. Hope I get one. There's a dance at Hopwood College on Friday. I'd love to go, don't know why — bored, I suppose. I feel like going to a dance all of a sudden.

I like Michael Fisher at school. He's really nice to me. I think he likes me. In the study rooms yesterday he threw me a book so that I could look at it. It was about the Rolling Stones. He just said, 'Hey, Margaret, catch!' I felt dead chuffed. He must like me. I don't think I'd mind going out with him, actually. It'd make school much more interesting, anyway. I wonder if he fancies me, or is he just being friendly? He's got fantastic brilliantly blue eyes when he laughs. It'd be weird going out with a boy in our class. It'd be summat different, anyway. Combat the boredom. When I think that I've got two more years to do in that dump, yes, DUMP, I could scream.

Susan Foster *is* a virgin. She likes to make us think she's not but she bloody well is!

Sunday, 15th November

I don't know why, but every Sunday morning I'm in such a rotten mood. I think it's Mass that does it. The same old bloody routine. Cornflakes, egg and bacon, cupsa tea, washing smalls, moochin' around, Sunday dinner — same feelings, same taste, same smell, every rotten Sunday. I think when I leave home I'll go to Mass on a weekday instead, 'cos I don't get anything out of Sunday Mass. It's only an occasion to show off. But very few people go during the week and it feels much more holy.

I wish I could talk to my brother Daniel. I wish I could talk to my mother. I wish I could talk to my father. Why not? The wall is so high and it's gettin' higher every moment of misery.

Monday, 16th November

In the corridor today when Mrs Hardwick said to me, 'Is there anything wrong at home?' I could've spat in her face. What does *she* know? Oh, Christ, is there anything *right* at home? Nothing except Nancy, and when she leaves to go to college, what'll happen then? I hate talking about home at school because I always end up lying. I hate it when Karen talks about her absent-minded mum. She makes her into a caricature and everyone laughs.

We've drifted apart, her and me. I can't talk to her like I used to. When I'm getting all the attention she tries to outdo me with her wit. She's funnier than me. Maybe that's why she's so opposed to me getting all the laughs. Karen

11

goes around with Lizzie Wisdish and Anita Baxter all the time now. Karen always sits and walks in the middle, with Anita and Lizzie on her either side. I'm extremely jealous 'cos Karen and me never used to be apart. Maybe that was half the trouble. Maybe it's because I'm a troublemaker and Karen is not. Maybe it's because I'm cheeky and outspoken and Karen is not. But she always manages to outwit me. She'll be a great columnist one day. I think she's basically honest but I think she doesn't really mind living at home, though she makes us believe she hates it.

Wednesday, 18th November

Karen never seems to go out or do anything, yet she always talks a lot. She's like Lizzie in that she doesn't go out at night and she's always smart and neat. She annoys me intensely when she comes out with comments like, 'I think all this underground and progressive music is a load of trollop', whereupon Lizzie immediately agrees with her. But maybe she says things like that for fun, to get me annoyed.

Faraday likes her and her crowd, or rather trio. And he shows it. She pretends she hates Smith, but I've watched her and she's all smiles and head-nodding in his class, like all the Smith Suckers. Maybe she's just good at covering up her feelings. I wish people would have the courage of their own convictions. It's like talking till the cows come home about someone then being as sweet as plastic sugar cubes to that person's face.

Mr Faraday doesn't like me. Mr Smith thinks I'm a cheeky little upstart, but Mr Denshaw doesn't know me. I think the only person on this earth who really knows me is Nancy. From her I've learnt to be cynical. Apart from the fact that I'm frequently called a cynical bitch, I'm glad I'm cynical. I'm glad Nancy is my sister, but soon she'll be gone, and then what? I've got 'friends' at school but I've got no *friend*. I think Karen might have become my friend, but I changed and she changed and after the metamorphosis we were worlds apart. We have different ideals, different morals, different tastes. I can't talk to her about boys or smoking or home.

Saturday, 21st November

> The need to be neutral
> not to be looked at
> not to be stared at
> not to be fancied
> not to be eyed up
> not to be spoken to
> not to be known
> wanting, needing nothing
> and yet so much.

I wish there was no need for boy/girl relationships. They're too tiresome, too much trouble, too complicated, too much everything. Why can't one just exist? Alone. Needing no one. Thinking nothing. Seeing everything. Wanting no one. I wish I had an ambition. I admire a hippy. Would that I could drop everything and start living. I wish I didn't want to be an actress. If I wanted just to be a French teacher, say, then I think I'd go far away for about five years and wander at will, meeting communes, viewing different scenes, and choose my own. Maybe that sounds superficial. I don't know.

Tuesday, 24th November

I wish I were neither boy nor girl. Oh, for the freedom of walking down a street and not being eaten up by the sex-starved eyes of lorry drivers. I wish men were not attracted to women. I wish men were repulsed by women. By me.

Why don't the straight younger generation stick up for their own generation? I hate straights! Straights are narrow. Straights are hard to spell.

Listening/experiencing Lennon/Yoko. Realising Lennon being. Realising Yoko being. Singing, recording, not caring, not knowing, just recording.

Bob Dylan is lovely. He makes me laugh. He makes me cry. I like Bob Dylan. I'm looking for a figure of . . . I do not believe in marriage, but maybe it's just as well.

Thursday, 26th November

The idea of living with my boyfriend while at college excites me. But what would I say? What would I talk about? What do you have to be like for someone to love you? Boys get bored with me easily. I don't talk, I act. I pretend, I put on accents. I can't communicate, I can't get through. I don't want *them* to get through.

Why do boys ask you out? It makes me so bloody sick. Why don't they just be friends and not ruin everything by asking you out? Why? Why can't we exist alone with the need for no one?

Listening to George Harrison. Does he know me? Does he see me? Everyday transparent. Flimsy in mind and soul. Maybe.

Saturday, 28th November

My every second thought is the fear of being pregnant. The stupid thing is, I don't know what happened. I don't exactly know what intercourse is. I don't know how long intercourse takes, what it feels like, what one has to do. I don't know what I'd do if I was pregnant. I couldn't stay here. My school career, my acting career, would be slashed down. I couldn't bear to face Dad or the people who matter. I think I'll go on a diet and see if I get any fatter. I beg, dear God, give me just a gram of your concentrated mercy and don't let me be pregnant. I think I would make for London if I was pregnant, and go and see Morag in the hope that she would help me without telling Mum or Dad. But, God Almighty, I implore you please to let me not be pregnant. I don't know whether it still only happens to the girl across the road.

Sunday, 29th November

I need a friend. I need someone to tell things to, to laugh with, to understand, to know, to see. I want a friend, not just an audience like my 'friends' at school. They laugh at my jokes but they don't know, don't care, don't see, don't hear, don't feel, don't understand. Claire tries very hard, but I don't allow. Somehow I feel she understands too many things and not enough. She listens, she imagines, but doesn't know, doesn't see through. She just lets me exploit myself stupid and renders me a transparent fool by her silence.

Monday, 30th November

I'm about to use a cliché: I'm sick and tired of school. No, really. Everyone says it but few mean it. School drags. Bores. I can't wait to leave. I count the days till weekends. I count the minutes till 4.15. At the moment I can't wait to go to college/university.

I think my parents read my diaries.

December

Your Stars for December

By the middle of the month you may well be faced with the choice of embarking on an intriguing romantic voyage with someone quite special. A confident and relaxed approach will get you furthest, but don't allow your head to be swayed by flattery.

Saturday, 5th December

Woodstock film last night was simple and beautiful, explaining so many things, revealing so many thighs but remaining beautiful. Some people got knocked down by the bandwaggon. A few survived. Mister James communicating to so many people and yet his inner human self remaining unheard. Lashing out rhythm and stomping away the beat . . . of his heart. The desolate wilderness of garbage was left strewn over the dry grass, listening to Mister James alone, surrounded by technical men. Fleshy bodies bathing freely. Joan Baez shown backstage a disappointment to me — she just like the rest. 'Ten Years After' loudly sensual.

Should be working but feeling queer, so I procrastinate.

Saturday, 12th December

Went to a party at Ruth Coombes' up the road. Sat on stairs all night talking to a boy who came from Enfield in North London. First year at Salford University. Lovely boy, lovely person. He was cynical about beautiful people and peace, brother, and Woodstock and trips, etc. I felt made, somebody was on the same level as me. Somebody else did not fit in at parties. He was young looking, plus black velvet pants. He wanted to say something at the end but didn't. He wanted to stay longer but didn't. He waved frantically, hidden in someone's car. I feel like writing to him but that would be pushy and pushy people repelled him.

And then Bob came (Rochdale Art College), dressed in black, and broke down the Londoner and mine's communication. Bob tried to talk seriously in the abstract. I don't

this is the hand that'll wear no ring

this is the hand that I
with I used for writing

this is the ha[nd]
with no wart

this is the hand
that can't expres[s]

this is the hand
that looks good
holding a cigarette

THIS
IS
MY
HAND !

this is the
hand that
looks awkward
when I'm
dancing

18

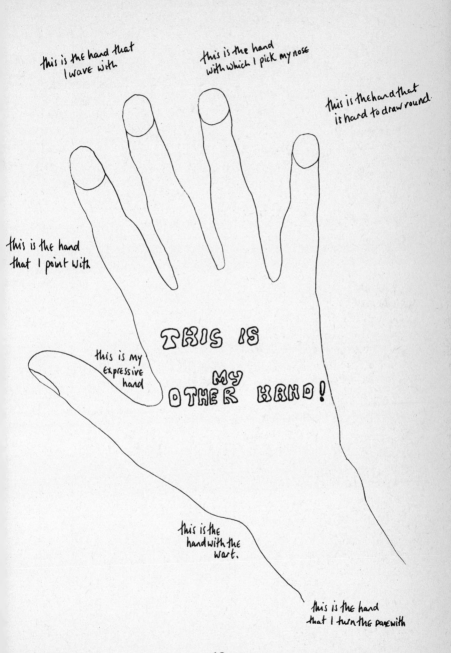

this is the hand that
I wave with

this is the hand
with which I pick my nose

this is the hand that
is hard to draw round.

this is the hand
that I point with

THIS IS
MY
OTHER HAND!

this is my
expressive
hand

this is the
hand with the
wart.

this is the hand
that I turn the page with

know whether he was clever enough to see through me. He liked me 'cos he had made little comments to me through the party. He wanted to 'go' with me, I think. Yeuk. Kisses at parties are too loose and not enough for me. He bent and kissed my forehead as he had to go. He said, 'Truth is everything.' But what is truth? Johnny Cash should be able to answer that.

Monday, 14th December

Everybody at school has got a fella but me. Can't see a time when I'll be going out with anyone before I leave school. Maybe it'll all happen at college. Get yourself a fella for Christmas! Saw Tina and Jacko, her so-called weirdo. It bitchily surprises me how she got him. Or perhaps she could talk to him. Yeah, maybe that's what it's all about. Too bloody vain. Susan Foster, thou complacent sot — or maybe I'm just jealous. I read today that black is not sexy. Maybe that's my trouble. I want an old fur coat.

Sunday, 20th December

Went to the Tim Bobbin pub and saw Roger, Baz, Shirley Connor and Trevor Saunders. Never spoken to him before but I had a drink with Shirley and then went back to the Theatre Workshop plus Trevor, who was rather drunk. He said he was only pretending. Sat on the bottom of the stairs watching the exhibitionists freak out into dance. Trevor came and sat beside me and started talking about the Bath Festival. He said he and his friend saw me and Nancy in a toilet queue there. He talked about Johnny Winter. He was getting more and more drunk. He kept telling me to get up and dance.

'I can't dance,' I said.

'You can,' he said, ''cos I saw you dancing in the Blue Eyed Devil.'

I wouldn't dance for him. I had to go at 11.30, and he

asked, to my surprise, if he could walk home with me. I agreed and so slung him over my back and set off. He clamped his arm around my shoulders. I didn't let him kiss me, 'cos I can't stand to be kissed by anybody drunk, so I left him with the agreement of seeing him again on Monday.

Monday, 21st December

Went to music lesson and then walked into town warily, 'cos I thought that he might not like me when he was sober. Got to GPO at just gone 8.00. He didn't come, so I walked towards Finnerties' and met up with him. I found myself talking really Lancashire. Went into the Red Lion. He put the *Sound of Music* on the jukebox as a joke. A man started talking to us, about the Rocking Vicars. He asked us if we'd ever heard of them. Trevor said no, but he'd heard of the Singing Nun.

I laughed.

I said I'd never taken pot, and Trevor said nor had he. I was surprised. He said he'd been scared, but he didn't really know why he'd never agreed to smoke any. He said, 'I'm sorry I'm so scruffy, but you look nice.' I felt over-dressed — too much jewellery, rings, bangles, etc.

Then we went in the Flying Horse. When we came out I asked, 'Are you bored?'

'Yeah,' Trevor said, 'but not with you. I sit there and I'm bored with the thoughts that come into my head. I live such a pathetically boring life.'

He asked me, could we walk home. I agreed. When we passed the bus depot he said, 'I suppose I ought to carry your bags.' I let him and then I linked him. 'Oh, I didn't know you cared,' he said. I felt queer linking him. When we got to the launderette he said, 'Can I see you again?'

'Do you want to?' I asked.

'Yes, 'cos I like you,' he said. It's funny when someone is

so frank. I was careful in what I said about my feelings. He kissed me and I agreed to see him on Christmas Eve.

Trevor Saunders. Green anorak. Greasy hair. Scientist. TEN GRADE ONES AT 'O' LEVEL!

Thursday, 24th December

Never been out on Christmas Eve before. Met him at GPO and went with him to pay his potato money in. We laughed together at the men in the office. Then we went to a pub and did the Salvation Army crossword. Went through the snow afterwards to the Two Ships.

'I was thinking of buying you a Johnny Winter record for Christmas,' Trevor said, 'but I didn't.' I was flattered. No boy has ever thought of giving me anything before. He asked, 'Do you mind if I get drunk?' I said yes.

Went in the Highland Laddie, then took a bus to a pub in Norden. I said I'd go to the bar 'cos I was less scruffy than Trevor. I turned round and the barman gave me the longest, filthiest look I've ever been given.

'I'll go,' Trevor said, 'follow me.'

We went round to the other side, whereupon a blonde barmaid asked, 'Is she eighteen?'

'Yes, of course,' I said.

'Good,' she said, ''cos we've got the police in.'

Trevor turned to me and said, 'Christ! We're really trapped. I know, run out now, just for a laugh.'

So out we ran, while the busty barmaid shouted, 'Here, where are you off to?'

We ran down to the terminus and caught a bus to the Golden Ball pub at Spotland Bridge. Trevor said, 'If I tell you how much I like you it won't be because I'm drunk.'

We went out of the pub at 12.05 and he put his arm round me as we walked home. He said, 'Can I see you again?' I said I was at the Theatre Workshop all next week. He said, 'Well, I'll see you a week on Sunday, then.'

22

'Yeah, but it's a long time, isn't it?' I said. We kissed and parted.

Monday, 28th December

Went to the Theatre Workshop all day, then the Tim Bobbin at night. Decided to go for my 10.40 bus. Was lonely and fed up. Walked to town with John Eastman who bored me to tears. Got on bus and sat on right-hand side upstairs, second seat to the front. Tiffany's lot were at the back of me. Found myself looking round to see if I could see Trevor in the town centre anywhere.

Suddenly Trevor's friend Martin Thorpe got on and sat in front of me. I was just going to ask him if he'd seen Trevor anywhere when Trevor sat down beside me. I was really surprised and glad and happy. He offered me a cigarette. His friend Martin turned round and talked to me. It was weird having someone whom you've seen for years on the bus and never spoken to, speak to you just like that. They had been out celebrating the fact that Martin had been accepted at Stirling University for Sciences. He said, 'So you are Trevor's *bird*, are you?' I laughed and yeuked. He was boisterous and merry and attractive (I must be true to myself in this diary).

Got off at our stop with Trevor and again my hair proved embarrassing when embracing in a kiss. God! I vowed out loud to have it shaved and cropped off.

'No don't,' Trevor said, 'I like your hair.' I was glad, and then we parted ways.

Wednesday, 30th December

Since Monday, being truth-conscious, I have to admit that I'm attracted to Trevor's friend. But I fail to see how him and me could make anything of it, he being Trevor's best friend and going away to university soon. It's a kind of status symbol, going out with the brilliant Trevor Saunders. But he likes me and I like him — if only Martin Thorpe weren't so attractive. Anyway, I can't wait to see Trevor again, so I'll see what happens at the party on New Year's Eve.

January

Your Stars for January

Now's the time for making those New Year resolutions. In matters of the heart resolve to tell the truth, you could save yourself a lot of trouble later on. Criticism may come at you from unexpected quarters this month, but don't fret over it; concentrate instead on the finer aspects of your life at present.

Wednesday, 6th January, 1971

When Trevor kissed me tonight he pressed me up towards him for the first time. I hope he thinks about me. His friends are pseuds. They cannot by any stretch play guitars. We laugh. We exchange glances. That's nice.

It's funny, I always used to say I couldn't go out with anybody unless I fancied them. If they weren't nice looking I never looked twice. Christ, how superficial! I like his mind.

> a white blossom
> a tiny moon as small and white as a single jasmine flower
> leans all alone above my window on night's wintry bower,
> liquid as lime-tree blossom, soft as brilliant water or rain
> it shines, the first white love of my youth, passionless and in vain.
>
> *D. H. Lawrence*

DH baby feels that when people have gone utterly sunless they shouldn't exist. Charming!

Trevor lent me his Johnny Winter LP. Played it at school. Some people grew to like it. Eileen Upton turned the volume down, mean pig. Trevor said to me, 'I was going to start smoking a pipe again but I thought no, 'cos you'll say I'm being trendy.'

Thursday, 7th January

I've got a friend. Trevor is my friend. Trevor is clever. Trevor gets drunk. Trevor likes me. My 'friends' at school are deteriorating into shapes in chairs, not listening, not looking, but most of all not caring whether I live or die. Christ, that was corny.

Friday, 8th January

Tonight was hell. Went to Coach and Horses with Johnny Winter LP to give it back to Trevor. Found him slewed out of his mind. Don't know why, but I started to become all actressy and nasty to him. Only for fun. He kept saying, 'Stop it. It's not right.'

'Okay, I've stopped, right?' I said.

He said he was sorry for being drunk but he had thought I wasn't going to come and so he had decided to get pissed. He asked me why I was being nasty to him, if anything was wrong. I said it was no use telling him when he was drunk. I told him he only puts his arm around me when he's drunk and so it means nothing.

We walked in silence to the Castle where he opened the door for me, which was strange. Went upstairs where there was a folk club in progress. Didn't stay long. Missed the last bus so we walked home in silence, with a wall between us. Sat on the wall at the bus stop.

'Would it help if I told you I was mad about you?' he said.

'It makes me feel guilty,' I said.

'D'you want to see me again?' he asked.

'Yeah,' I said.

'You can tell me to get lost if you want,' he said. 'Don't just say "yeah" 'cos you don't want to hurt my feelings. I mean, it worries me when you say "yeah" 'cos I always wonder if you really do want to see me again. If you say "No" I'll probably cry, but I won't kill myself.'

'Oh, thanks!' I said.

He laughed and told me, 'Come in the Coach and Horses tomorrow night and I won't be drunk, okay?'

I now realise that my behaviour towards Trevor was due to feeling insecure. Trevor opening doors for me, saying

27

'I'm mad about you', saying 'I could apologise for anything to you,' etc. was weird, 'cos nobody has ever felt anything for me before, it was completely new to me. I was nervous and to cover up my nervousness I was bitchy and nasty. Perhaps.

Saturday, 9th January

Went in Coach and Horses and saw Trevor sat on his own looking sullen. Hilary Lucas and Christine Anderson were in with their respective boyfriends. Didn't say a word to each other for a long time except stupid things like, 'What've you been doing all day?' etc. Felt embarrassed because everyone else was talking away and having a good time and we just couldn't speak to each other. In my own superficial way I thought that I'd tell him what was wrong last night and then it would be all right. He said, 'Drink your cider and then we'll go.'

Went into the Red Lion. He said, 'It's bad, isn't it?'

'Yeah,' I said. I wanted to lean against him and cry.

'Maybe if we get the cause of the trouble out into the air by talking about it,' he said, 'it'll be all right.'

Eventually I told him what was wrong. I said after, 'Logically I should be happy 'cos a boy says nice things to me.'

'I wish I could understand,' he said. 'Y'know, yesterday when you said jokingly, "self, self, self, that's all you think about", well, I think it's true that, because when you tell me about things that are bad with you I only think about how they're going to affect me in relationship to you. I'm too immature, aren't I?'

I asked, 'Why?'

'Because I should be able to comfort you and I can't. I don't know what to do.'

'What could you say?'

'That's just it, I don't know.' Some women put 'I love you because you understand me' by Val Doonican on the jukebox. God, how ironic. Watching the women round the jukebox, Trevor said, 'If I were happy I'd think, what marvellous people, 'cos they're enjoying themselves.'

'But you're not happy,' I said.

'No,' he said. 'Shall we go?' So we went.

Outside the pub he put his arm round me. I felt glad and loving 'cos he wasn't drunk and he'd put his arm round me. It meant something. I felt protected. I put my arm round him for the first time. Went to the Castle and he made me laugh so much talking about his mum and dad I nearly wet my knickers. Walked home after. Went into a chippy. It was the first time I'd ever been in a chippy with a boy before.

When we got to the launderette he said, 'Have you had a good time?' I said truly yes. He said, 'Yeah, you've said some nice things to me tonight. Like when you said, "You're about the most mature person I've ever met".'

'I hate using that word' I said.

'I don't think I've said anything that I'll regret tonight', he said. 'Usually I say things, then I think, Christ, what did I say that for?'

'Like what, for instance?'

'When I said I'm mad about you. What a stupid thing to say! I mean, it's ridiculous, isn't it?' I hope he meant it, though.

He told me to come in the Coach and Horses on Friday. I thought, it's a long time to wait, but didn't say anything. He's going to bring his Stones LP on Friday so I can borrow it. He kissed me and pressed me close to him. He said, 'Usually I go home crying to myself but I won't tonight.' I think we were both glad.

> I think about him
> I hope he thinks about me
> I think he thinks about me
> I like to think about him
> I think I like him.

Friday, 15th January

Trevor said he feels inferior to me! If anybody should feel inferior it's me, 'cos I'm so thick and superficial.

Saturday, 16th January

Met Trevor at the station and caught the train to Manchester. He said, 'I've opened up my character to you but I'm not going to let you know everything about me.' I said that I was scared he might be taking the mickey out of me sometimes and taking me for a ride. He said, 'I couldn't take the mickey out of someone I feared,' which was strange. He said he was fascinated by my facial expressions, that he liked my eyes. I don't know whether he was joking or not. He said, 'How come that everything I do turns out a failure?'

Trevor made me laugh on the train by telling me about his Aunty Molly. I desperately wanted to lean on his shoulder but couldn't. Don't know why.

Didn't talk much on the way home, felt moody and tired. Told Trevor that I couldn't talk. He said, 'Talking is sometimes irrelevant.' I asked him whether he talks about me. He said, 'People ask me things like, "Are you still going out with Margaret?" and, "How's Margaret?" etc.' He said that Colin said I was a typical girl because of the way I talked to people. I was dead annoyed and upset and angry that Colin had made a snap decision on my character just like that, without even knowing me. Trevor told me to come round to his house on Wednesday at about half eight, to collect his Stones LP and Johnny Winter LP. It'll be strange going to his house, but I'm excited at the prospect.

Trevor said that he's lost two and a half stone these past few weeks. Yes, he certainly does look thinner. He's got blue eyes. I noticed at last.

30

Wednesday, 20th January

Went, having told Mum where I was going, round to Trevor's at about half eight. Listened to records and his sister made us a cup of tea and some toast. Trevor's hair was greasy. Went down to the Golden Ball but by the time we got there it was closing time — my watch had been slow. So we walked back up home.

Some girls that used to go to Trevor's school were at the bus stop and so he just said, 'Well, I'll see you, then,' and he never kissed me. I was glad, really, 'cos it would have been embarrassing. But all the same it was embarrassing him making a point of *not* kissing me.

Friday, 22nd January

Went to Coach and Horses. Trevor was sat in a corner not talking to anyone. He said, 'Let's go somewhere else.' So we went in the Red Lion. He said, 'Y'know, when we were walking home last Saturday I thought how great, we don't have to talk, it's just all right. And then you went and ruined everything by saying how you couldn't talk.' But I'm glad he thinks we don't have to say things.

Saturday, 23rd January

Met Trevor at the station and I ate my chicken sandwich on the way to Manchester. He said to me, 'It's nice hair, that.' I was flattered. 'D'you notice anything different about me?' he went on. 'I've washed my hair.'

Got to Manchester and we had to queue up for the film. Felt embarrassed. Everybody was being so very obviously trendy — everybody was very hairy and arty and we were all going to see the film because it was about young people and drugs. Oh God, how pretentious. It made me laugh.

More was chronic, it was about nothing, just a boy's

31

progression from pot to heroin to death. No more. No depth. They had a cheek to call it Germany's *Easy Rider*. I was embarrassed at first seeing a boy put his hand up a girl's skirt and between her legs. But it just showed how much of a flesh market the world is. Trevor said the words were corny as well. He was bored and tired. Sixteen bob down the bloody drain. The girl, Estelle, was beautiful — sun-bleached hair, brown, lean body. Music were by Pink Floyd. They might as well not have bothered.

Went for a drink after, then for the train. Went in the first class compartments and stuck our feet on the seats insolently. All around girls, victims of the pick-up-flesh society, were deject and crying. After getting all dressed up they end up in tears late at night.

Some lads were talking about who owed who a drink. They went on endlessly. Trevor said, 'See. It's better not to talk at all than talk about stupid things.' I agreed.

I asked him later on, 'What's up?'

'I'm just feeling sorry for myself, that's all,' he said.

I asked him why but he shook his head. I said, 'Why won't you tell me?'

'Would it be too corny if I asked you what you think of me?' he said.

'Do I know what *you* think about *me*?' I said.

'I should think so, yeah!' he said. He thinks and worries a lot.

Had to phone Dad at Rochdale to tell him that I'd be late 'cos someone had pulled the communication cord on the train. He said, 'Where are you?' I said, 'Rochdale Station.' He said, 'How are you getting home?' I said walking. He said, 'Walking? It's pouring down. Stay where you are, I'll come for you.' I protested saying, 'It's all right, I've got an umbrella, Dad.'

Realised when I came out of the telephone box Dad would see that I was wet through when I got home, and he'd say, 'I thought you said you had an umbrella.' Was frightened and kicked myself for telling lies. Got home dripping rain droplets, but Dad was in the bath so I was saved.

It's been a month. It's just been so. No big argument. No scenes. Just us. Is it enough? We've been a month.

Tuesday, 26th January

Days drag, lessons bore, it's a long time till Friday. Think on him a lot these days. Just hope it'll be all right. Helen Kilpatrick is very good looking.

Friday, 29th January

Went in Coach and Horses and saw Trevor. Martin Thorpe came soon after. Trevor was drunk. Thorpey made me laugh. He kept looking at me. Went in Flying Horse and tried a Tia Maria which was really horrible. Wouldn't let Trevor kiss me in the pub — don't quite know why.

'Ignore everything I say 'cos I'm drunk but I do love you,' he said. 'I'm happy now 'cos I'm with Thorpey and you, and you're the best people around.'

Walked home with Thorpey and Trevor. Felt myself wanting to link Thorpey so as not to make him feel out of it, but didn't.

Saturday, 30th January

In the Coach and Horses tonight when Colin said, 'Eh, why don't you come up to our school some time? You'd enjoy it, wouldn't she, Trev?'

'No, would she 'eck,' Trevor said quite emphatically, which was strange. Didn't quite understand why he was so opposed to the suggestion. Later, when we were in the Red Lion, he said, 'I've been reading the Sermon on the Mount today.'

'Why?' I said.

He said, 'Just so I could tell you I'd been reading the Sermon on the Mount.'

I wonder what Trevor says to Thorpey about me. Was nasty to Trevor on the way home, but only playing. Went in the chippy and laughed. Trevor asked me to come to his house on Wednesday so I'd have another opportunity to practise my nasty remarks on him. I laughed and left him kicking the wall in despair.

February

Your Stars for February

Communication is the key to all successful partnerships. Worrying and wondering does you no good at all. Try and deal more directly with your partner. Speak your feelings clearly and simply, remembering always that he may be as new to the game of love as you.

Wednesday, 3rd February

Went with Trevor on the bus in to town and into the Coach and Horses. Embarrassing 'cos it was really quiet and people were almost whispering to each other. Went out soon after. Went in the White Lion on Yorkshire Street opposite Cheetham Street. Didn't talk much. Went home on bus early, about half ten. Trevor said he's going to Manchester on Thursday to get tickets for the Johnny Winter concert and so I gave him a pound for my ticket. I was a bit put out at having to pay for myself. Parted. Wondered why he'd asked to see me on Saturday and not Friday. Wondered why he'd asked to see me again at all, 'cos tonight was quite boring, really.

Friday, 5th February

Went to Theatre Workshop at night for an hour to see what was going on. Saw Trevor on the way there as I was going to the bus stop. I said, 'Where are you going?' and realised that we had acted just like mere acquaintances. Was worried. At about half nine I was sat on the bus in town, waiting for it to go out, when Thorpey and Trevor came round a corner. Thorpey pointed up to me and waved, but Trevor just sort of looked up and carried on walking over to the Coach and Horses. Was mad. Wanted him to tell me to get off the bus and come in the Coach and Horses. Was worried about whether he thought, Oh bloody 'ell, look who it is!

Saturday, 6th February

Work was incredibly tedious and draggy. Went in the Castle at night. Saw Trevor sitting with Kevin and girl,

Colin, Rick and Lynne, Martin and Gerry (reading a book and looking nice). Trevor apologised for the presence of the crowd. I sat silently. Kevin's girl kept staring at me. Surprisingly, she's not bad looking. Nice hair. Lispy mouth, though. She and Kevin were holding hands—God! Later they all left except me and Trev. Atmosphere was strained and I decided to ask him why he'd asked to see me again, what he thought of me, why he'd ignored me on the bus last night, etc. He said he couldn't understand why I was asking all these things.

'Did you plan that you were going to talk like this to-night?' he asked. 'I don't know why, but I sensed it was going to be like this: you sitting there talking like that and me crying to myself. I just like being with you, that's all.' When I asked him why he'd asked to see me again—habit or what?—he said, 'I'll always ask to see you again.' He was annoyed and chain-smoked.

'I'm sorry,' I said.

'Yeah,' he said, and went to the toilet.

Later we walked down Manchester Road in complete silence. Along the esplanade he stopped at a bench and sat down and I did the same. Was shivering wildly and he said, 'Can I have a cigarette, please?' Sat there for about a quarter of an hour, then he said, 'Shall we go? I feel better now. I've sorted it all out.' He was suddenly elated.

We carried on walking across town and up Drake Street. Went into the Citizens' Inn opposite the Odeon. It's where all the teddy boys and Italian greasers hang out. Was almost deserted. A kissing couple in the corner being intently watched by two Italians, and three wrangler-jeaned youths fiddling about with the juke box. The room was blue lit. It was like some seedy pub out of West Side Story or a Graham Greene novel.

Trevor pulled out a ticket for the Johnny Winter concert and just sat there staring at it. We were the last to leave. His eyes were watering and he said it was because of the smoke. I asked him why he was chain-smoking. He said, 'I'm worried, aren't I?'

'Shut up,' I said.

'I am! It's been the most emotional experience in my whole life.' I didn't know whether he was joking or what. His eyes were still watering.

Walking back along the esplanade he was a mixture of tears and smiles. I was mixed up, didn't know what was going on. I said, 'What's up with you?'

'Don't yer know?' he said.

I said, 'No.'

'Course yer bloody know,' he said.

I said, 'I don't, I want to know.'

He said, 'Well, it would seem that this is the last time I'll see you, so walk slowly to make it last longer. It's all I've got left.'

I said, 'So you thought I'd come out tonight thinking, Right, I'm gonna finish with him.'

'Yeah.'

'Well, thanks a lot!' I said.

'I'm sorry,' he said, 'but that's what I thought.'

'Well, it's going to be pretty embarrassing when you ask to see me again.'

'Why? Cos I'm gonna ask you!' as if he was threatening me.

'Well,' I said, 'it'd be pretty pathetic if I had to say "No" at the end of all this, wouldn't it?' From that he deduced that I would see him again.

It was all right in the end. We were friends again and we parted with me saying I'll come to his house next Saturday night. We're gonna see *Easy Rider*.

Sunday, 7th February

When I think how before I wanted to have a big argument with Trev just for the sake of having an argument, 'cos all couples (yeuk) are supposed to argue and fall out, but NOW! Christ, how superficial I must've been! I'd never want to go through Saturday night again.

Monday, 8th February

I don't want to say what I really think about Trev, nor do I want to appear too amorous, because then he will have got me and he'll know how I feel. Somehow I don't want him to feel secure and safe, knowing how I feel about him. Don't know why but I want him to keep worrying about whether I like him or not. I feel that when I've said 'I love you' to Trev and he's said that to me, it'll be over. We'll be there. There'll be nothing left. It's a strange feeling.

Friday, 12th February

Am frightened that me with Trev might become a weekend thing 'cos I only see him then, which is bad 'cos I have time to think during the week. There are times when I think, Oh, I wish Trev were here, and so wanting him to be there during the week makes all my emotions get cooped up inside me, and when they are released at weekend it is in either one big flood or in one long, moody evening. It's bad. It's unnatural. But I can't see him at night during the week 'cos of homework and Dad, so what else is there for it?

Must tell Trev to grow his hair longer at the sides. I wish I could talk to his friends. I always think that Trev is embarrassed because I never say anything when his friends are there. It's a bit like the shyness that comes over me when I go to the Theatre Workshop.

I keep wondering why Trev hasn't asked to see me on Fridays lately. Perhaps it's because I never say a word when we're in the Coach and Horses with his friends and so I'm perhaps a nuisance or embarrassment. Or perhaps it's because he doesn't want me to be bored by going in the Coach and Horses every Friday. But then, why couldn't he go somewhere else with me on Fridays? Or perhaps he prefers his friend Thorpey to me. I think he does and I don't blame him.

39

Saturday, 13th February

Went to Trev's house and then to see *Easy Rider*. What an eyeopener! The ending was shockful and full of impact but people got up to go (as they knew it was almost over) so as to escape the rush. God! Some people! They mustn't have thought about it at all. I was hit. I was knocked by the sheer unfairness of the Easy Rider's lot in life. And then to end it all they shoot him. It's as if they're getting rid of the embarrassment, shoving it under the carpet, or rather into the grave. People in the flicks couldn't give a damn. It was just another Saturday night film to them with a bit of music thrown in.

Went in the Navigation Inn. Bought some chips after and ate them sitting in a doorway, 'cos it was hailstoning. Trev told me on the way home that when he was nine he used to cry because he knew that he would die in a few years and so would everyone. He said he couldn't understand how people could laugh when they would soon be dead. He said, 'I don't think I've told anyone that.' I thought how honoured I was.

We smiled and laughed before we kissed each other, which was nice. He said, 'Farewell.'

Monday, 15th February

Went to Trev's in my yellow mac, all the time wishing I'd put my long black one on. His Dad took us to the station. Went in the Café Royal when we got to Manchester, then over to the Free Trade Hall which was pretty full. We had good seats and Thorpey came when Formerly Fat Harry had just started.

I don't know why, but Trev seemed annoyed. Thorpey wanted a light off Trev and Trev said, 'Oh, fuckin 'ell!' Weirdly annoyed! Went out during Formerly Fat Harry 'cos they were boring. Thorpey, Martin and Gerry came out as well and we went up into the bar.

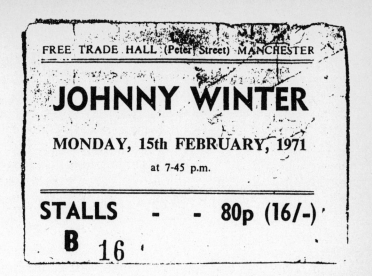

FREE TRADE HALL (Peter Street) MANCHESTER

JOHNNY WINTER

MONDAY, 15th FEBRUARY, 1971

at 7-45 p.m.

STALLS   - -   80p (16/-)

B 16

Thorpey said to me, 'How's Trev? He's in a bad mood, in't he?'

I said, 'Is he?'

'Yeah,' he said, 'din't yer know? It's very subtle, yer see.' It worried me that Thorpey might think, Well, she doesn't know him very well.

Went back in for Johnny Winter. I feel myself sometimes flirting subtly with Thorpey. He's very good looking, funny and quick-witted — and yet there's Trev. Why is it with us? Is it just status? Do I feel special 'cos he likes me, whereas he doesn't like girls usually? Do I feel special 'cos Trevor Saunders — the clever, cynical Trevor Saunders — actually likes me? Oh, Christ, what is it, then? I know it could never happen — me and Thorpey — totally impossible. But do I want it? Thorpey goes out with girls for a fortnight's laugh and then gets bored. But is it *the fact* that I could be going out with someone (Trev) for a long time that is so attractive?

On the train coming home I was extremely tired, but although I told Trev that I was tired he kept offering bits of conversation. Yet usually he says, 'We don't need to talk, do we?' Could hardly keep my eyes open. It worried me intensely that I couldn't get involved with the rock music and that I couldn't let myself go. Felt full of inhibitions. Felt embarrassed because everyone around was stamping their feet and shaking their heads and yet I could only sit there and watch. I kept thinking, No, this isn't me. The people at school think if anybody will freak out it'll be me, but why couldn't I? Because of Trev?

'Was it an anti-climax?' I asked him.

'Yeah, it was rather,' he said. 'I didn't get involved personally with the music. Mind you—I didn't really expect to.'

Why couldn't *I* let myself go? Me, without any inhibitions! It was so unnatural for me to be sitting there hardly moving, or was that the real me and the inhibitionless Margaret Onions is just another actress?

Trev's dad was at the station and he gave us and Thorpey a lift home. I was in the middle of Trev and Thorpey in the back. Trev asked me whether I was coming to his house for coffee but I said that I'd better go home.

Trev seemed to be half sulking in the car. I felt that he was jealous or annoyed at Thorpey's presence. Trev's dad dropped me off at the end of Sandy Lane and Trev just said, 'I'll see yer, then.' Christ, I didn't know what to say, so I just said, 'Yeah, I'll see yer, ta-ra!' Thorpey had to get out to let me out and he seemed to have a puzzled expression on his face. I don't know whether he was thinking, What the 'ell is Trev playing at? or what. I was stunned. It may have been because his Dad and Thorpey were there.

I remembered then that on the train Trev had asked me if I'd like to go and see *The Magic Christian* at the Film Theatre. And I remember now last Saturday's events. He might have just said, 'I'll see yer, then', to give me a taste of my own medicine—he thought that I was going to finish with him last Saturday and so he was perhaps saving himself from the pain that he would suffer if I were to have finished with him tonight. In other words, he might have just finished with me so that he'd finish with me before I finished with him. I don't know what to think. I want to know what he'll say to Thorpey about me. But I thought people only said, 'I'll see yer, then', to one-night stands. I think I have a right to something better.

I think I'll leave it over the weekend and see what happens. If nowt happens I'll go to his house on Monday and ask him about it. Nancy doesn't think he's finished with me. I hope Thorpey's not there when I go round on Monday.

Friday, 19th February

Saw Trev standing in the No. 9 bus queue when I got off the bus, and we just looked at each other for a long time while I walked past with Lizzie Wisdish and H. Kilpatrick. I expected him to say quickly: 'Come in the Coach and Horses tonight, will you?' But he didn't say anything, he just stared.

When I got home the phone rang and it was Trev phoning from Royton after he'd got off the No. 9 bus. He said he was just wondering why I'd ignored him when I was walking past the bus queue. I said (because I didn't want to talk as Dad was there), 'Shall I come and see you? Tonight or Saturday?' He said, 'Saturday'd be best 'cos I'm going drinking tonight.' I was a bit put out because it seemed that he'd rather go drinking with his friends than see me.

Anyway, I went off to the school dance suitably attired in jeans and yellow mac. Really 'freaked' out (oh boy!) at the dance. Loads of girls in hot pants — yeuk!

A girl in the loo said to me, 'Eh, are you Margaret Onions?'

'How do you know my name?' I said.

She said that a mate of hers had told her about this Margaret Onions who was right freaky and weirdo.

Back in the hall I danced outrageously, jumping high, rolling over, lying down, sitting down. A boy put his finger on my head and said, 'Get up!' He put out his hand and pulled me up. It was Lawrence Wheeler! Lovely hair, quite long. Fantastic dancer. Kept coming up and going away. I said, 'I hope you're not taking the mickey.' He said, 'No, I'm not.' It was great. We were the only two dancing like that.

The song finished and so did the dance. Lights up and embarrassment. Walk away. Lawrence walks away with Julia Moran English-Rose-Virgin-look. I nearly died. They were so incongruous!

Lawrence kept talking to me and playing at the bus stop. He's gorgeous-looking, but that's all.

Saturday, 20th February

Met Trevor and went into the Red Lion. Jokingly I said, 'Oh, by the way, you owe me ten bob.' He said, 'What d'you mean?' He took it seriously and worried about it. Left the pub at about 11.15. Walking along the esplanade Trev kept lagging behind so I kept waiting for him to catch up. He didn't look at me at all. Suddenly I turned round and he was walking away from me and turning into the memorial gardens. I followed and found him sitting on a bench with his head in his hands. Crying, I think. Didn't look at me.

Confusion. No idea what to do. Didn't say a word. Wanted to say, 'What's up?' but I thought that he'd rightly expect me to know what was up. I thought how bitchy and remote and sarky and impersonal I'd been and wanted to say 'I'm sorry,' but just left the silence to itself. Didn't stop at the launderette but just went our different ways without a word.

Christ, what drama! He's bloody deep and sensitive and renders me a heartless bitch by his one-sided vulnerability.

Thursday, 25th February

Went to see Trev. He ended up apologising for Saturday night, whereas it should have been me doing the apologising. Didn't stay long. I expected to go out for a drink but we didn't. Went at nine o'clock.

'Are you coming round some time?' he said.

'Are you not particular whether I do or not?' I said.

'Yeah,' he said, 'I want you to come round. Come round tomorrow at about quarter to nine, all right?'

Friday, 26th February

Nancy got on the same bus as me and Trevor going into town. Trevor at his best on the bus, smiling and joking. Nancy laughed and so did I. Went in the Wimpy Bar for the sake of a change. Went in the Citizens' Inn after.

'D'you like this,' Trev said, 'just sitting in pub after pub?'

'I don't mind,' I said. 'There's nowt else to do.' He was happy, I could see that.

Went in the Red Lion after. Trevor put his arm around my waist tight and said, 'It's been right good tonight. You've been really nice and I can go home feeling happy now. Do you realise you have bad moods when you're nasty and sarky? I've been timing them, seeing if there's a pattern which might be due to your female physiological processes. Then when you're nasty I can think, Oh, it's all right. I know why and I understand.

'You must take into consideration that you're my first girlfriend,' he said. 'I find it strange. You're too important to me. I should just be able to think when you're being nasty, oh, stupid girl, and then not bother, but I can't, you matter so much.' I loved him for that then but didn't say so. He asked, 'What do you think about going out with boys? Do you think: Oh well, I've got as much as I'm going to get out of that one and then move on, or what?'

No, that's not what I think. Those were very crude terms. We kissed more than usual, which was good and not routine like.

Saturday, 27th February

Stayed in all night. Trev went to queue for the Stones tickets.

Went round to Trev's house at about half eight. He looked tired and worn out. He told me about queuing up for tickets. Said he only got one ticket. Said he was going to sell it.

'You could give it to me,' I said.

'No, could I 'eck! That'd be stupid.' He mentioned ethical objections.

'What ethical objections?' I said. He wouldn't tell me. Called him a swine half-jokingly.

He laughed and said, 'Oh, shut up. You're like a baby wanting a toy: Can I 'ave it, can I can I 'ave it?'

Went to Coach and Horses later. He told me his ethical objections. He said that he thought it would make me think of him as a pathetic creepy and feeble person if he gave me the ticket after having stayed out all night for seven hours in the snow and freezing cold. He said he thought it would be a more masculine and admirable (from the female point of view) thing to do if he kept the ticket himself. He thinks and worries a lot about what I think of him and that worries me. It frightens me.

'I reckon you're going to get the ticket in the end,' he said.

'Why?' I said.

'Because you've got too much power over me.' I don't know whether he was joking or not.

When we were walking home he said, 'Well, it's turned out nice again,' which was quite witty, actually. He made me laugh, talking about the potato firm men and their plumpest, leanest sausages in town. It embarrasses me because usually we only kiss each other when we're saying 'Ta-ra', which is bad. It shouldn't be like that. And the fact that he only puts his arm around me when we're walking home. I often want to get hold of his arm and link him or something, but I'm scared of what he'll think. It's still remote and formal. It's verging on the platonic.

March

Your Stars for March

There are a few emotional surprises in store for you this month. Beware of cryptic conversations: they could cause even more turbulence in your private life. Your tendency to bottle things up leaves those close to you baffled as to your true feelings. Try not to judge those around you too harshly; tolerance is the key to harmonious relationships at both work and play.

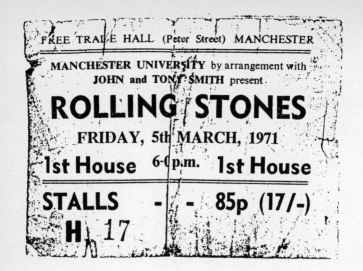

FREE TRADE HALL (Peter Street) MANCHESTER

MANCHESTER UNIVERSITY by arrangement with
JOHN and TONY SMITH present

ROLLING STONES

FRIDAY, 5th MARCH, 1971

1st House 6-0 p.m. 1st House

STALLS - - 85p (17/-)
H 17

Friday, 5th March

Stones concert. Different to Johnny Winter concert somehow. I became involved. I stamped, clapped and cheered and shook. Mick Jagger outrageously beautiful in pink satin. Shed his jacket for 'Satisfaction'. Shook his hips incredibly for 'Honky Tonk Women' and stormed on with 'Jumpin' Jack Flash' like some precocious child actor. For 'Midnight Rambler' he took off his belt and whacked it round the stage. They were only on for an hour and so we all shouted 'More' for ages, but they didn't come back on — probably because they're supposed to be anti-establishment!

Went in Coach and Horses after, when I got back to Rochdale. Trev was stone drunk. Didn't quite know how to take it. I went to the loo and when I came back he'd gone. Tony said, 'He's gone outside. Shall I go and see where he is?'

'Is he really drunk?' I said, and Gerry told me how Trevor had drunk half a bottle of whisky. I said, 'Oh he's a slob, isn't he,' and Colin said, 'Ah, but yer love him, don't you.' I didn't answer.

Trev came back in, white as a sheet. He'd been sick outside. I was mixed with embarrassment, annoyance and repulsion. He took a pill for bad breath. God, I was nearly sick with repulsion. He kept getting hold of me. I felt uncomfortable. I said, 'I want to go home on the bus.'

He fell asleep on the bus. I was in a funny mood and didn't speak. He let me go before him getting off. I didn't want to kiss him, I just said, 'Go home and sleep it off.' Don't know why, but I couldn't bear him to touch me. I'm a very repulsable person. I must be.

Saturday, 6th March

Bought a pink blouse from the Oxfam shop for three bob. Went to Trev's at about half eight. Felt queer and not in a talking mood. Felt annoyed. He kept saying, 'What's up?' Went in two pubs and didn't speak. He said, 'I wish you'd say something.' Went in the Red Lion. Was still moodily silent.

For some reason I said, 'Wouldn't you like to find yourself another friend?'

He said, 'No, why?'

'Don't you think it would be better?'

'Do you think I'd be happier? Well I wouldn't. I won't find myself another friend. I know I won't.'

'What d'you mean? How d'you know?'

'I just know I won't.' After a bit he said, 'Would you like to?'

'I don't know,' I said. 'Sometimes I just wish there was nobody around me all the time, just me, and that I didn't have to go out with anyone.'

'I don't understand,' he said. 'I wish you'd put it another way in simpler terms. It sounds as if you're thinking about my benefit, and people don't usually do that. I find it hard to believe that you're just thinking about my benefit and not your own.' He was saying that I was caring about how it would benefit him if we finished. I hadn't meant it to go so

49

far. He took it to mean that we'd finished. Tears rolled down his face. He looked at me and said, 'I wish you'd say something. If I understood I'd feel better.'

'You just make me feel a heartless bitch, that's all,' I said.

'No,' he said, 'I don't think anything worse of you. I may do in the future, but I don't now.'

Went out the pub and walked in silence. He kept walking closely to me and I wondered what he was trying to say. After an age I said, 'Is it too late?'

'Too late for what?'

'To carry on.'

He put his arm gently round me and said, 'No, it's not too late, honestly.'

He caught hold of me and kissed me and hugged me. I felt frightened that I was responsible to such a great extent for his feelings. He was really happy all of a sudden, and relieved. I didn't deserve to be treated how he treated me. He should have slapped my face. I was amazed that all I had to say was, 'Is it too late to carry on?' and suddenly we were back together again and he was hugging me and almost thanking me. He said, 'Are you sure you want to carry on? Because I've always thought that you weren't getting anything out of it and I was.' He asked me whether I was only doing it for his benefit. I said 'No,' but I wondered and thought that that was half the reason. He said:

'It would be better if I had a more take-it-or-leave-it attitude, don't yer think?'

'Better for you?'

'For you as well.'

I tried to think myself into that frame of mind, but I couldn't. I nearly said, 'It would make me feel less responsible for your feelings and therefore much happier,' but I didn't.

I wonder, when he said, 'I won't find another friend,' whether he meant ever in his whole life or at the moment, in the immediate future.

50

Sunday, 7th March

Daniel came home with Joanne — good looking but funny clothes, short patterned zip-up cape, waistcoat and skirt. Funny laugh. Daniel looked good in black flared trousers and dark brown jumper. Mum made the classic boob when she said, 'Come on, Bre-Joanne, you can sit here.' Oh boy! I don't think Daniel noticed, though. Did not go round to Trev's at night.

Tuesday, 9th March

Helen Kilpatrick would not go round Manchester with me this afternoon 'cos she had her uniform on!

Wednesday, 10th March

Had a peculiar-in-the-extreme feeling all morning till I went to catch the bus. Like one of my weirdly scaring dreams — awareness of my every breath, every move every sound, frightening. Big argument blew up at school because the positions of the football team had been decided upon by three members of the team when nobody else was there. No bloody democracy. Gina K. couldn't see that it was because of the principle of the matter. She told me what she thought of me in front of everybody. Felt horribly lonely. Everyone has a particular friend who waits for them at quarter past four, saves them a place on dinners, etc. It's because I'm such a bloody swine in their eyes that I've got nobody; people don't want an outspoken laugh for a nice, cosy friend. What duff Lower VI girls we've got — so boring, so good, so dutiful, so practical, so sick. I'm aware of my loneness every time I walk across town to the 11C bus stop. I feel as though everyone knows I'm on my own. I don't want any of Lower VI girls to be my friend anyway, they're too dull.

Friday, 12th March

Went with Nancy-looking-beautiful to the Theatre Work-shop to see *All My Sons*. Went past Martin Thorpe and Co. in town and Thorpey couldn't take his eyes off Nancy when we were walking past, even though he was supposed to be saying hello to *me*.

Saturday, 13th March

Went to Trev's house at night. His sister opened the door and said, 'No, he's gone out.' I was stunned and angry and indignant and scared. Went in the Wimpy Bar 'cos I couldn't think of anywhere else to go. A tramp with an American accent and an old man, both stark-raving bonkers, sat on either side of me and talked. I've never felt so much like crying in all my life. Nowhere to go, nothing to do but talk to those two. God, how callous and selfish! Went home at ten o'clock.

Sunday, 14th March

Trevor rang and asked me to come round in afternoon but said I'd come round at night because of homework. Went round. Asked me about my eye make-up. Felt embarrassed. He'd washed his hair (for me, so he said — oh yeah, sure!). Said he'd been drinking.

Went out to the Highland Laddie. Trevor had his green windjammer on and looked nice. Went in Coach and Horses, San Remo and The Queen's. Told him about the football match I'm playing in, between Lower VI and Upper VI. He said, 'Oh no! I wish you hadn't told me that.' Said I'd ruined my image.

In the Coach and Horses Trevor said that at first he had got the impression I was very conscious of the fact that I was a girl. I remembered Colin saying that I was a typical girl. Trev admires people like Germaine Greer and other liberators. I was annoyed at the impression he'd got of me. Maybe it's true. Wanted to tell him of my writings on wanting to be neutral, but didn't. Kept thinking that he can't possibly know me if he thought that.

'You don't like people, do you?' Trevor said. 'I know what you meant when you said you want to be on your own sometimes. In fact, I think I know exactly what you meant. Having thought it over I can understand now. I didn't at the time 'cos I was slightly intoxicated.' (Last Saturday.)

Will see him in Coach and Horses on Friday. Must not wear any eye make-up. God, how superficial and false and appearance-conscious! *Ora pro nobis!*

April

Your Stars for April

Question time this month for you Taureans as you try to make sense of the world around you. On the home front there may be difficulties, but a calm, sensible attitude will see you through. Your love life will be subject to your close scrutiny this month too, but delay doing anything radical until you've had time to really think things over.

Friday, 2nd April

Went to see *Performance*. Good film but sat too near the front. Had headache. Came home last train, couldn't talk, felt moody and tired. Never can talk on last train, can't stand Trevor's dad taking us anywhere. Makes Trevor look weak and young and pampered.

Saturday, 3rd April

Went on a 15-mile walk for school in aid of St Joseph's Penny. Walked with Claire. Every step was agony. Talked to Claire about me and Trev. She said, 'When you love somebody you want to touch them and hold them all the time.' But then me and Trev — I don't know. Decided that it's too much of a one-sided thing between us. I don't put enough into it. Can't finish it before his 'A' levels, though, 'cos I'd upset him terribly. That sounds bloody smug but I think it's true. That's the whole point: he shouldn't be like that. He should treat me rough and like dirt instead of almost putting me on a pedestal, 'cos the pedestal is only made of gravel. It'll soon crumble when the rain comes. He'll realise I'm just a feeble bore.

Sunday, 4th April

Morag and Miroslav came home. I wanted to cry. Mo and Miro, Nancy and Dave, they're all so bloody happy. I believe that sex *does* count. Not actually sexual intercourse but sex *appeal*. Think that's one of the things missing with me and Trev: I just don't fancy him. God, it sounds bloody awful but I believe you have to be sexually attracted to someone *as well as* mindly attracted in order to have a complete relationship. Will there ever be a good combination?

Monday, 5th April

Have decided to buy an old fur coat on my birth-day. Have also decided to slim. Really slim. **S** Gerard Bailey is playing Romeo to my Juliet. Am not **L** very pleased. Can't see any romance about to **I** flourish in the Summer School. I am braless. I **M** am liberated. I wish I were — I just feel floppy. Saw Cathy Lomax in town. Beautiful. She's had her hair feathered. Still beautiful. She must be rather small. Looks tall. She's lovely and skinny. She had a tapestry twenty-pound coat on. Helen Kilpatrick has gone to Corsica for Easter. She'll be beautiful and brown when she comes back.

Easter Monday, April 12th

Nancy went to Gerard Bailey's party last night with Dave. I went to bed early. Suddenly my tears burst out in choke-fuls. Could not hold them any longer. Morag and Miro, Nancy and Dave, all so bloody happy. I ate to fight off the boredom. Felt fat. Lay on my bed in knickers and jumper. Morag came up and said, 'What's the matter?' Then I burst out in jugfuls. She put her arm round me and said, 'Don't cry, tell me what's the matter.' Told her I was so bloody miserable. God, it was weird having her comforting me like she was my mother. It was nice. I loved Morag then. She did care. She was my sister. I wanted to throw myself into her arms.

Lying there on my bed last night I was overcome with *the*

56

most intense jealousy of Nancy. Having someone like that living with you, it's impossible to live with yourself. Plus the fact that she's nice to you as well! I realise that she could not possibly have it better: good looks — long, beautiful hair, big dark brown eyes, small feet. God, she's just too good looking. Clever, intelligent, witty, good speaker, a leader, popular, good actress, confident. Christ, she can't go wrong! And on top of all her inexhaustible qualities, she always gets the best boyfriends. I know that sounds petty but it's significant. Her boyfriends are always the leader of a group. She's been at the Tech College since September and in the first three months Keith Waters, Mike Jordan and Dave all wanted to go out with her. She picked the leader and the best — Dave. She's had an opera written for her by Joe Buxton, she's had a poem, 'Call her moon child', written for her by Jim from Liverpool — what else?

God, I'm so eaten up with jealousy. But how can I have any confidence when she's around, in the limelight, in everybody's eyes and mind? How do I stand a chance? I can just imagine this year's Summer School at the Theatre Workshop. When the audience see *Romeo and Juliet* they'll automatically think Nancy's Juliet and I'm the mother. She's smaller than me, younger looking than me, prettier than me. Everyone will be saying, 'Nancy should've been playing Juliet. Why isn't Nancy playing Juliet?'

I think I'll tell her to play Juliet. I know I can't do it, I haven't got it in me. All this stuff about being a versatile actress doesn't apply to me. I'm just not the girl to play Juliet, I'll ruin it. I bet Gerard Bailey wishes Nancy was playing Juliet. They'll be discussing me when I'm on stage. Nancy would've had ideas and different interpretations of scenes, but I won't: I'll stand there with no ideas and nothing new — just boredom. I don't want to play Juliet.

I bet Trev thinks I've finished with him. Oh God, I don't know what to do.

Saw Anna George in church. God, she's beautiful. Lots of eye make-up. Skinny. Just beautiful.

Nancy was on the Oxfam fast with Gerard Bailey. Nancy went to Gerard Bailey's party last night. Nancy's gone to Gerard's today to watch *War and Peace* on BBC2.

Ethel next door never stops saying, 'Eee, I do think your sister's a bonny girl. You can tell you're sisters. Mind you, she's a thinner, smaller and more delicate version of you.' But she never says anything about me being pretty. Well, does anybody? Dave just about managed to say, 'She wouldn't be bad looking if she tried.' Gee, thanks! Even Trev never says anything about my looks, so I can't be anywhere near pretty. Morag once said, 'You've just got to accept the fact that Nancy is the shining light of good looks in our family and lead your own life.'

God, I feel so big and clumsy when I stand next to my sisters. I feel so bloody ugly and awkward. When anybody says anything complimentary to me I always think that they wouldn't say it if they saw my sister Nancy. Anna George is my beauty idol, Nancy is my ideal girl. I think I might adore her if I wasn't so jealous. Christ, when I walk down the street, through town, through Manchester, anywhere, it's always Nancy that catches people's eyes and minds. Martin Thorpe couldn't keep his eyes off her when we walked past him, even though he was talking to me. Jagger . . . is getting married!!! Ugh!

When I think that this life is just a corridor through which one must pass in order to get to the important and everlasting world beyond, what does it matter that you become famous and a good actress in this world, what's the point? This world is only a fraction of one's whole life. And yet you *must* use your worldly life to its best advantage. You mustn't waste it. Why can't I drop everything and become a hippy in, e.g. the Californian mountains? I want to act, to work in the theatre; I couldn't do that if I was a hippy of no fixed abode.

Why is it that if one went and joined a commune it would be taken for granted that you would smoke pot? Why, if you're a hippy, must you smoke pot? Why is it a necessary

58

feature of hippy life? I'm just plain scared of the stuff, seeing as I get stoned on cigarettes! I can't walk straight for a while. I go dizzy and my head feels funny, and that's just with tobacco. Christ, I'd probably take off if I smoked pot! Yet at university/college if you smoke pot you're automatically 'in the group' or whatever. It's a companion acquirer. What's wrong with pot, anyway? Pot is top of the pots. Pot makes you potty like a spot makes you spotty.

> Tall fat girls don't look good.
> Small fat girls are not as noticeable.
> Small thin girls look good.
> Tall thin girls look fantastic.

Bloody 'ell, that lot sounds like something out of a women's magazine. I don't give a damn, I'm going to be thin! Like that!

Tuesday, 13th April

Went to Mass tonight. It was good. Only about eight people there. It was private and holy and peaceful. Went to communion for the first time in ages. Felt awfully pious. Came out after and felt wonderful, cleansed, liberated, soulful and full of peace, freedom and wholesomeness.

Friday, 16th April

Went to meet Trev in the Wimpy Bar. I got there first and he came in later. He was tired. I was in a happy, don't-carish, talkative mood. He said I was in a 'silly' mood. I felt like saying, 'I am me. Take me as you find me,' but I didn't. Went in the Coach and Horses after. Trev asked Jim Lyle to bring some shit (pot) in on Saturday night so that he could buy some. Trev said to me that he only asked Jim in order to see how easy it was to buy shit in Rochdale.

'Would you smoke it with me?' he asked. (Safety, security, guiltless in numbers, thought I.) 'Would it lower your opinion of me if I smoked the stuff?'

I said, 'Would it matter to you if it did?'

'Course it would,' he said.

I said I wouldn't smoke the stuff with him. Rely on yourself, your body elements, Tchaikovsky Piano Concerto No. 1, empty churches, walks alone, 'Jumping Jack Flash' at full volume, a real good freak-out at dances once in a while, etc. etc. But I'm not prejudiced against people who do smoke the stuff.

Went out of Coach and Horses at 11.10 pm. Oooh, how precise we are! We were walking along the subways when Trev said he was going to sit down on the next bench 'cos he was tired. I said 'okay'. But then I said that I was going to carry on walking while he sat down for a rest.

'Why?' he said. 'Why won't you sit down?'

'You sit down because you are tired', I said, 'and I'll walk 'cos I'm not tired, OK?'

'No. Part of the wanting to sit down was wanting to sit down with you. I want to walk home with you more than I want to sit down.'

But no, I wanted him to sit down 'cos that's what he really wanted to do and it was stupid to sacrifice his rest for the sake of walking home with me. I can't stand being on pedestals. He thought it was something personal. He said, 'I'll worry about this, yer know. And about what you think of me — 'cos you never say.'

I said (truthfully?): 'It doesn't mean anything to me about you.' It wasn't that I wanted to walk home without him but a matter of principle: he wanted to sit down so he should sit down.

Sunday, 18th April

I realise more and more, as time passes quietly by, that our relationship verges on the platonic. I feel frustrated. It shouldn't be like this. We should be able to touch one another at any time: to hug one another; to hold each other's hands; to touch each other — that's all. I feel I'll never find anyone to love who is as deep as Trev is, yet do I love Trev? I think not. I wonder if he feels the need to touch me and yet is inhibited. I can't stand the routine 'goodnight kiss'. God, it sickens me — he never kisses me at any other time. Our shoulders don't even touch when we sit in pubs.

Christ, maybe it's me! I don't think so, though, 'cos I've never been like this with anyone else. Maybe it's me who's being frigid because it's him and not Terence Stamp.

Monday, 19th April

Back at school. I keep thinking that it's because I'm Trev's first girlfriend. God, he almost adores me. It's peculiar. I can't bear to think of the fact that he's a virgin. I like men to be all experienced and full of know-how instead of just 'beginners' like me. God, I'm bored. I never kiss him properly (French kissing). I wonder why not? I wonder if he thinks I don't know how to kiss properly. I wonder if I'm the first girl he's ever kissed. I can't see Trev going out with another girl after me.

I wish I didn't like him so much. I just wish he wasn't so nice. If he was bloody horrible to me I wouldn't think twice about finishing with him. Usually it's me being mad on a boy and the boy not caring two hoots about me. I wish he didn't think I was so special. He overestimates me. I don't have to work for anything or try or strive for anything with Trev. I feel stagnant. Brigitte Bardot realised, after reading Jean Paul Sartre, that she only loved her present husband because of the image he had of her — she loved *the fact* that he had a fantastic image of her, she didn't love *him*.

Have written to Littlewoods and Marks and Spencer for Saturday jobs. Hope I get one.

Tuesday, 20th April

I don't want to play Juliet. I'd much rather play Lady Macbeth. I'd be able to do her much better than Juliet. I just can't play a young and beautiful fourteen-year-old girl in love. Nancy would be ideal, and I know everyone else thinks so, too. Mind you, I've got to do it well so as to get a good reference off the director.

We had a political view assessment of ourselves today in General Studies, a test to see whether you are a socialist, conservative, fascist, etc. I turned out to be a tough communist.

Wednesday, 21st April

Last night my dream was of lesbians. The two of us — watching TV adverts with lesbians in them. I fulfilled, satisfied, climactic extremity. Physically felt when I awoke. Outrageous. Frightening. Talking to Tina about going to Italy with her next summer. Hope the possibility is realised into concrete. Engaged girls violently repulse my very soul.

Friday, 23rd April

Went babysitting with Tina, and Jacko her boyfriend came. When I was leaving Tina whispered to me on the front doorstep, 'Well, what do you think of him?' Christ, that girl! Went to meet Trev in the Wimpy Bar. He'd been waiting for over an hour. Went in the Flying Horse but didn't talk much. Didn't talk going home.

'There's something happening, isn't there?' Trevor said. 'Why am I walking along saying stupid things and you're not saying anything?'

Christ, I kept thinking I must be a lesbian or frigid or something. I can't stand it when he says how stupid he is and how everything that he does fails. I can't stand it when

I see him as being inferior to anyone or anything. I want the strong one, the omnipotent.

'If I didn't want to go out with you I wouldn't,' he said, 'and if you don't want to go out with me you shouldn't. I'm obsessed with thinking that you don't really want to go out with me but you are doing so as not to hurt my feelings.' It's true that I'm not happy going out with Trev, but I couldn't finish with him before his 'A' levels, it just wouldn't be fair. The thing that got me about that 'Play for Today' was, when that lorry driver made a pass at Julie Driscoll, she just fought him off, saying, 'No, no, look—I just don't fancy you, that's all.'

Trevor said, 'Have you anything to say?'

I said, 'I'll go in and I'll come and see you tomorrow.'

Saturday, 24th April

Went round to Trev's house. He gave me a book of poems for my birthday. Went to Wimpy Bar. Did not touch me all night. Did not kiss me. Almost platonic completion now. Don't know if I like it. Tina told me that Jacko said that he hadn't expected me to be as attractive as I was!! It's good with Tina, every time we see each other we just burst out laughing.

Sunday, 25th April

God, I'm seventeen today! Every day I grow more and more afraid of growing old and never growing young again. My book of poetry is nice. Ezra Pound Selected Poems. Nobody has ever given me a present like that before. I like Trev tremendously as a friend. But I think I want it to remain platonic. Think it is platonic now, but I'm not quite sure. I think I might even love him as a friend. I'm confused. Must sort it out, see what he thinks about it. Wonder if he thinks it's platonic? Summer School at the Theatre Workshop with Gerard as Romeo and Trev watching will be peculiar.

Nancy loves Dave so intensely it's beautiful. Hope she gets into Central, she'll get to know this week. I really hope she does. I keep thinking about how much I'll figure in Trev's past life when he or anyone else looks back to it.

Nancy told me today that Andy Tomlinson said that my smile really knocks him out. I was really chuffed, but deceived a little, I think. Anyway, what are looks?

Tuesday, 27th April

I don't know, if Trevor and I carried on this platonic thing, whether I would feel queer going out with another boy. I would hate to lose him as a friend. He's a fantastic friend, but I just don't phancy him. It's not physical. I don't know what to do. I don't want to finish with him completely 'cos then I'd lose his friendship. But if we carry on as platonic I wouldn't be able, or I wouldn't feel free or right, going out with other boys. I'd feel as though I was being unfaithful. I'll have to ask him about our relationship. I wonder what he thinks. Does he think I'm frigid or something? Nancy thinks that he might be in love with me or infatuated with me. She thinks that he is thinking, This is it. She's the only one for me, etc. He hasn't touched me for weeks — mind you, I have to say I haven't touched him. Why can't it be normal?

Nancy told me last night that Morag is getting married next Easter. We are going to be bridesmaids! God, it's so final. I'll have a married sister! Yeuk. Nancy told me also that Daniel doesn't believe in marriage. Funny, I always thought he did. She said she doesn't think he'll ever get married. Wonder how long Joanne will last. Nancy says she doesn't like the way Joanne makes it so obvious that she and Daniel are living together. Nancy says Joanne is too blatant about it for this house. It's peculiar having a brother, and knowing that your brother has sexual intercourse with his girlfriend. I hope he won't end up being a bachelor of about 35. God, that'd be unbearable. I reckon he will get married. Don't know why, 'cos I won't, certainly. Wonder if I'll be a virgin forever? Wouldn't like to be on the pill the first time I had intercourse with someone. I'd like it to be completely natural and not plastic. So don't know what'll happen. Anyway, who would have me?

I realise I was only 16 when I went to the Bath Festival. An enormously vast pop festival at 16 years of age! I *must* go to the Isle of Wight festival this year. But who would I go with? Nancy will be with Dave. Not Trev, couldn't go with him. No girl at school would go with me — not that I want them to, anyway. Can you imagine that lot at a pop festival! They'd have to be having washes every two minutes. They'd stare at people with long hair. Christ, they're so damn narrow and protected. Bloody Catholics!

I'm getting nervous about drama school auditions already. Want to apply for RADA and Central acting courses, not teaching courses, 'cos if I'm not intensely interested in teaching I'll not study it intently, so I might as well try for a course in which I'm intensely interested. Hope with all my might that I'll get in. The higher you aim the more you fall. Who am I talking to? Myself, I suppose. Who else would listen?

May

Your Stars for May

Getting the balance right is always a difficult task, especially for you Taureans with your love of neatness and order on the one hand, and your desire for anarchy on the other. Travel and financial prospects look good for you this month, so take time off and allow yourself to indulge in a favourite fantasy or pastime. Whatever you do, don't let indecisiveness spoil your fun.

Saturday, 1st May

Have now got £10! Two fivers! Met Tina in my lunch break. She told me that Jacko had said I would suit his friend Stan perfectly, 'cos we're both outrageous and loony-like.

Went to meet Trev at night. Went in San Remo coffee bar. Susan Foster and her crowd came in. She looked at Trev as if to say, who's that? She whispered to me, 'Is that Trev?' I said, 'No!' Left the San Remo and changed my mood and acted daft and messed around. Kept getting on buses and getting off before they set off, for a laugh. Walking round and round bus stops and lamp posts.

Trev said, 'I can't understand you. Why do you behave like this sometimes and not others? Let's go somewhere.'

I said. 'Where?'

'Smith Street lavatories,' he said.

'You're learning,' I said. So off we went to Smith Street lavs.

When I came out he was sat on the steps. We then walked up parish church steps and sat on a bench. Sensation of utter peace. Calm, noiseless, peace on a mountain. Silence. Dusk. Far from the vacuum of noise and screams and drills and crying. Told Trev how I couldn't stand someone who used to see me around town, someone who has formed an image/impression/idea of me in his mind, getting to know me. It detracts. There is no distance left any more, no mystery, no curiosity. He knows what I'm like now. He's heard me, seen me, watched me, listened to me. I can't bear anybody getting to know me. I don't want anyone to know me.

Trev didn't understand. He tried to, but language and words were the obstacles. As they are now. Later, when we were walking down parish church steps, he said, 'Anyway, you know me and nobody else does except my brother.' I felt good but felt terrible and fed up and bored and annoyed at nowt. Trev said, 'Your shadow on the pavement is familiar to me now. Arms folded, hair out and coat flapping.'

Went in the Red Lion where Trev told me he's going to live in London in September. He said, 'If I do go to London can I write to you?' Wonder what'll happen when he goes. What will his letters be like? I'll tell him to write first. Wonder if he'll change with being in London.

'You know how I'm badly affected by my "A" levels now,' Trevor said. 'Well, I think after my "A" levels I'm going to be a lot better, and it would be awful if you had only known me when I was in a sort of long bad mood.' I knew he was trying to say, Don't finish with me for a long, long time, let's carry on for a lot longer.

Trev told me that Thorpey fancies Ella Jackson. He's a born flirt. He also said to Trev, 'She's all right, Margaret's sister, isn't she? How old is she?' He's at it all the time. It's sickening. All the same, it makes me miserable to think that he doesn't fancy me. I wonder if he does?

Saturday, 8th May

Have bought an old second-hand fur coat. Dark brown coney, midi length. Big enough for a pregnant lady. Met Trev in Wimpy bar. Wore my fur coat and boots. He was wearing some new baseball boots. They looked really clean and new. I laughed. They looked funny. Can't tell whether he likes my coat or not. He said he wouldn't come and see *Romeo and Juliet*, 'cos if I was bad it'd be embarrassing, and if I was good it'd still be embarrassing.

Went to the Duke of Wellington after. Felt sick and came out. Sat on a bench in Cenotaph sunken gardens. Beautifully peaceful. Tulips lit by lamps. Silhouetted cherry blossom gently swaying in the breeze. Red Lion later. Sitting next to him, I got a feeling of really liking him. He said that he didn't think I was easily influenced by trends or by people. He meant it as a compliment, but if only he knew how influenced I have been by various people and things.

Later he said that he hadn't been to school all week.

'Have you done any work?' I said.

'No,' he said, 'because I couldn't get out of bed.' That was really funny, I laughed a lot at that.

Can't forget my immense fear of growing old, growing up. Nobody bothers about the middle-aged and the old. Everybody talks about the young, everybody wishes they were young. Maybe it's the limelight bit that I don't want to lose. God, I'm eighteen next birthday. Time rushes silently by. I'm frightened. Don't want to be the older generation. Couldn't stand being old and seeing all the young people about. Intense jealousy. People say, 'You'll accept it when you do grow older, you'll adjust in time,' but I don't think I ever will. Can't stand to think that I might even think like an old person.

Tuesday, 11th May

Don't want to be settled with Trev as my one and only. So early. Don't want it to be a boy/girl relationship. Want it to be a person/person friendship. Hope he wants it that way. Though I think I would be intensely jealous if he went out with someone else. I'd still like to go drinking with him.

I wonder what he thinks when I don't kiss him good-night. I wonder if he'll want it to be completely platonic. It's platonic now in the sense that we rarely touch or kiss each other. Yet he looks and talks to me as though he was my boyfriend, as though it was a normal boy/girl relationship. It's half and half. I don't know where I am.

Gonna see *Loot* on Friday. Have to meet him in Wimpy at quarter past eight. Must write to Morag. Hope Mum and Dad will pay my fare to London. Am excited. Travelling will be the best part.

Thursday, 13th May

Off school with a terrible cold. Feel rotten. Am dying to go to London. Fare on coach will be £2.65 and I'm going on the 9.20 coach from Rochdale on Sunday morning, 23rd of May.

Sunday, 16th May

I'm afraid that when Nancy goes away to college I'll stay stagnant, not advancing, perhaps retreating. Want to keep with her, in touch, but I know we won't, it'll never be the same. She'll meet lots of fantastic people and I'll just become her dull, sheeplike sister. If I weren't me I'd like to be Nancy. The perfect one. The honourable. A person about whom people write poems and operas. I don't blame 'em. Oh God, what a mess I'll make of Juliet.

Trevor keeps saying, 'In five weeks my "A" levels will be over forever.' He's making too much of it. He thinks that when his 'A' levels are over we'll be all right, we'll be better. He thinks it'll be great between us. I'm afraid about the negative possibility. I find I'm possessive about D.H. Lawrence. I don't want anybody else to read his poems.

I realise I love Nancy. She—I don't know, but, God, I love her. She's so high up and me so low. She deserves Dave, everything. She warrants it. Where can I find a friend? Will I ever? Cathy Lomax is beautiful—olive skin. Nancy told me she's going out with Jim Keating, the beautiful, black haired, blue-eyed swine who lives in the town flats. I want to be as thin as Driscoll. Beyootifull Jools!

For the past fortnight I've been undecided whether to travel down on the coach as the sex bomb in tiny black dress and high heels and low-cut neckline, or as the hippy who's left home. I love playing at not being me. I'm so boring. But have now decided, seeing as Morag is meeting me, that I'll have to travel down as plain dull old me. I wish my hair would grow.

When Nancy didn't get into Central Dad said, 'I still say they want their heads tested.'

What d'you mean?' I said.

'Not accepting her,' he said. I realised how good he must think she is. But she is, isn't she? I wonder whether he thinks I'm any good or not.

Tuesday, 18th May

Can't remember whether I wrote about the programme about lesbians when it was on. That affected me greatly. Firstly, it made me infinitely more tolerant. Why not? It was beautiful at the end—a party with women and girls all dancing together to the soulful beat of the recording of 'Lonely Days', by the Bee Gees. I can understand them. Why shouldn't girls in love walk down the street hand in hand?

Sunday, 23rd May

Journey by coach to London and Morag's college. Two boys got on at Manchester and sat on the next-to-back seat. Me on the back seat. One boy blond, green eyes, faded denims, brown hands. Me, while readjusting my seat, made a noise—squeaky with the seat—and laughed; boy turned and smiled/laughed. First in series of turns and looks/smiles. Other boy very quiet—presumably the other's follower.

Got to Derby for dinner. Got off coach. Pub over other side of road. Blond boy walked slowly and looked at me a long time before going into pub. I walked further up the road. Turned round and ended up in same pub. First words spoken. Silly words, e.g.:

Him: 'Why didn't you come and sit over here?' (Yeah, why didn't I?)

Me: 'Why didn't you come and sit over here?'

No more talking. The two left. Blond boy nodded and

71

said, 'See yer.' Knew long before that he fancied me. Me him, too.

Got back on coach and two girls had got on. Bang goes my chances, thought I. Turns and looks yet again. Coach sets off again. I thought, 'I'll be pushy for once! Well, why not? So at the next look I motioned him to come and sit next to me and talk to me. He sort of said with gestures, 'I can't.' Oh, no! Embarrassment multi-dimensional by failed attempt. But then he got up and came and sat next to me. Conquered. Got him. Done it. Cockney accent. About 19, from Harrow. A draughtsman. Talked about his mum as 'the old lady'. Funny being chatted up again, not been for ages. He thought I was leaving home to come to London and live. Didn't tell him otherwise. Would have liked to kiss him. Wonder why not? Perhaps he didn't fancy me close-up. Who would?

Coloma (Morag's college) meals laid on, linen changed weekly, rooms cleaned daily, Morag's friends are real. So nice but not falsely so. They really are her friends. Morag very popular.

Friday, 28th May

I've got a job at Park Cake Bakeries for Rochdale holidays — £11 a week plus £1 on Saturdays = £12 per week. Met Trev in the Wimpy Bar. He told me that he won't see me for three weeks because of his exams. He said, 'It's going to be pretty bad, seeing as how I'm dependent on you.'

Suddenly I became moody and silent and depressed and sad. Nowt to do with anything, I just turned sad and depressed. Trev kept touching, putting his hand on my hand, hand under my chin, hand on back of my neck, trying to ask me what was wrong. Wanted to scream out, 'Nothing physical, please!' Couldn't bear him to touch me. He felt a bit hopeless too, I think. Went outside. Trev stopped and put his arm round me and put his head against mine. I said, 'Don't, please.' God how cold and stonelike of me. But I want to be able to be miserable and then happy the next minute without having to explain it to anyone.

Trev's planning to buy a motorbike in the very distant future. Don't think he'll ever make it. I've realised I'll never achieve my ambition of riding at 100 miles per hour, on a 650cc motorbike along the M1 with no clothes on, with the wind and sun rushing all through my body. Exposed to the bare elements. Trev asked me to come and see him in three weeks' time. I agreed. Must tell him after three weeks about lack of want for physical side. God!

June

Your Stars for June

If you find you've got more time to yourself this month, try and use it not just for quiet reflection but for getting out and about a bit more. Take a break from the intensities of one-to-one relationships and look around at how others organise their lives. You may pick up some useful tips. On the fun front your secret longing for freedom of physical expression could find an outlet on or around the 18th.

Saturday, 5th June

Am fed up with staying in. Saw Michael Fisher on the bus across the road after work today. He gave me a big smile. He says my name nicely. I think he fancies Alison Leigh, though. I think I like him. I don't know what to do about Trev. Christ, where am I? Where am I going to? Exams next week. Haven't done a stroke as per usual. Jud (Tina and Jacko's friend) who looks like John Lennon, is having a house-warming party next Saturday. Would not mind going!

Tuesday, 8th June

In English, if Faraday is late for the lesson, the class talks and entertains itself. The girls turn round and the boys make us laugh. Sounds Victorian! Anyway, if Michael Fisher is talking he seems always to direct his attention to me, with a few diversions, just to bring the rest of the class into conversation. 'Hey, Margaret, etc., etc.,' talking to me in particular. I wonder if other people notice it.

Thursday, 10th June

Had a dream last night, almost a nightmare. Oh, God. I was reunited with Trev. He tried to make it 'normal'. The kissing repulsed. Slobber. On top. Almost real. Believed in it. God, it can't be 'normal', after these three weeks I couldn't bear it! I won't allow it! I couldn't!

Saturday, 12th June

House-warming party in Castleton. Never been to a more lousy party in my entire natural! Paul (owner of house along with Jud) gin drinker, not bad looking but too smooth, not scruffy enough, fancied me outright. I acted the goat. Acted mad. It worked: 'I've seen some weird chicks in my time but she was crazy' (Paul) — Tina told me what he'd said. He wanted me to stay but we left.

Monday, 14th June

First day at Park Cake Bakeries. Feeeeeet! It's funny, it seems a long time until I see Trev again. These three weeks are really dragging. Didn't think they would. Thought I'd enjoy the solitary feeling.

Thursday, 17th June

Fourth day at the jam and cream factory. Pay day tomorrow. They all think I'm a Cockney who's left home and is living with mates in a flat in Rochdale and waiting to go to Art College in Liverpool. It started with a Cockney accent and with it came a character and with that came a new person. I think differently, I have a different attitude to things, I really live the part of the Cockney girl up North. At the moment I'm using Easy Tan from Boots and feel good and brown. Would you believe olive skinned! Ann, a permanent worker at Park Cake Bakeries, talks about her two miscarriages as if they were grocery items which fell out of her shopping basket. She's been there for six years! After four days at the place I'm ready for off. They deserve a medal. God, are they the country's heroes!

Friday, 18th June

Doreen, the Supervisor at Park Cake, is going to South Africa with her minuscule husband — 'Mind you, as I say, I won't be nasty to them darkies 'cos like I say it's their country int it?'

Went round to Jacko's at night with Tina. Listening to

76

records and feeling bored. I said jokingly to Tina, 'Let's go into the kitchen and take all our clothes off.' Half and hour later there I was sitting about stark naked! It was glorious, free and open. I lay on the floor outstretched. Defenceless! Tina wouldn't take hers off. She only went as far as her petticoat. She said I've got guts, she couldn't help but notice them. I wonder if Jacko will tell anyone. Hope so. What a reputation for me! Yippeee!

Nancy is still in the Lake District — post-exam elation. I hope Trev's exam results are good. Miro writes letters to Morag because he can't afford phone calls. His letters are long and full of poems to her.

I have exactly twelve months before I leave school.

Saturday, 19th June

Met Trev again and went in the Castle. He's got an interview in London for a job at the university or something. He was wearing a new jacket and new jeans. He looked good. Saw Barbara Davies with Gordon Wood. She must be mad — he's horrible. Miriam Langton has got a nice fella, looks about 22. Fragile is she. Unique voice. Artificial? Just because my Cockney accent is artificial I suspect everyone else of being untrue.

Sunday, 20th June

Nancy has returned from the Lakes. She didn't even sleep in the same tent as Dave! She got a letter from an old flame when she got back. He wants her to write to him. She's going to. Wonder what'll happen. He still makes her heart throb frantically, I think. First love and all that rubbish. Dave gave Nancy red roses for her birthday. I just thought, if Trev gave me red roses I'd be repulsed. I'd hate it. Must study *Romeo and Juliet*. Nancy's just told me she did in fact sleep in the same tent as Dave.

Saturday, 26th June

Met Trev in town and he told me he'd got the job in London, something to do with examining after-births and blood. Saw Linda Buckley in the Castle with her fiancé. God, he's horrid. Matching tie and handkerchief. Too old. She had an engagement ring on. Relationships are good in so far as they are a proof of one's existence. Trev said, 'You do realise that most of the time when I'm philosophising I'm speaking tongue-in-cheek, don't you?' I didn't answer, so he said, 'Course you do. You realise everything, you do.' He said he realised that the only thing he talked to me about was his troubles. He says he's going to try and stop it. I smashed a bottle of Guinness against a wall going home.

Monday, 28th June

Jacko, Tina's boyfriend, told his mate Jud about the nude night the other week. Jud said about me, 'Is that the one with the hair and the pumps? When's she coming again? So he's noticed me! Gooood!

July

Your Stars for July

You Taureans may be famous for enjoying domesticity, but being ruled by Venus, you're always on the look-out for sensual delights. This could be your lucky month for chance meetings, but be careful what you say on the 9th. If you speak or act without thinking, disasters or disappointment and confusion will result.

Thursday, 1st July

Romeo and Juliet rehearsals have started. First scene with Gerard. First kiss. Not too repulsive, thank God! Needs to be more lively. Sullivan, the director, said, 'This play is going to be the best thing I've seen so far — I decided that a long time ago when I chose you.'

Saw Trev after rehearsals in the Wimpy. Didn't talk much. Too tired. He kissed me. He was so depressed and miserable I felt he needed to kiss someone so I allowed him to use me as an object. I wanted to scream out, 'Nothing Physical, Please! It can't be. I don't want it. It won't be!' I value his friendship so greatly, I don't want us to stop being friends. Why can't we continue just as friends? Why did he have to go and kiss me? If I go out normally with boys when Trev goes to London I wonder if I'll tell him. Would like to visit him. Am dreading writing letters to him. People are different in letters, they sound strange. He'll wish he'd never known me. I can't write for toffee. Must go and see *I Am Real and So Are You* at the Library Theatre in Manchester tomorrow.

Friday, 2nd July

Got paid £13.14 including tax rebate from last week. Went to Manchester straight after work. Bought a black blouse with silver-white embroidered flowers on it. Got to Library Theatre early. Sat on steps in foyer and an African man tried to pick me up. I'm not a whore, am I? Came out after two acts. Bored rigid.

Came back to Rochdale and saw Tina, Jacko and Jud in the Bowling Green. Jud a disappointment. Looks better far off. He rolled a fag on a street corner. Immediately shut myself off in an American accent. He does not deserve to know how boring I am. I'm so ordinary and uninteresting. Yes, you are a bore! He thinks I'm meeting him in the Bowling Green next Friday at eight o'clock, but I don't think I'll go.

Saturday, 3rd July

Met Trev in Wimpy. Went to Castle and stayed there all night. It was a good night. Good moods. Thank God he didn't try to kiss me. Think he wanted to, though. Felt drunk after one and a half pints of cider. Thought I could see the sun going down — midnight. It was the moon! Aunty Lil and Uncle Boris were in the pub. My God! Why must we have relations?

Sunday, 4th July

Went to Workshop. First scene with Gerard again. *He's* going out with Julia Moran now.

Monday, 5th July

Workshop with Nancy. Hard to look her in the eye on stage. Because if I'm Juliet and she's my mother, when I look her in the eye I become me.

Tuesday, 6th July

Workshop with Diane Moody. Boring account of her holiday in Spain. No good at improvisations. I stayed behind to do the balcony scenes with Sullivan. I half fancy him in an absurd sort of way. Except his ears. But his voice, powwwwwwwww!

Dad said to me today, 'You and I are going to have a chat soon, my dear! (so bloody formal) I believe you are expected to get two Ds and an E for "A" levels, which are

81

no bloody good to anyone!' That's a lie. Smith would have said I'd get an 'A' in French. But, God, the way he approaches me! My heart sinks and I immediately shut myself off when he comes in.

Thursday, 8th July

Saw Trev in Wimpy after school. Tina and Jacko came in. Sunbathing hopelessly at school. Michael Fisher is away. Dull. Nobody to smile at. Said I'd see Trev on Saturday. My pumps are rotting.

Friday, 9th July

Went in Bowling Green. Jud did not appear. Empty. Sat in a good place so I could look in from the outside. Black cloak, black jeans, brown bare feet. Distant mood. Filled up quickly. A group of three lads in the middle were talking. About me, I believed. I was right. One came over and said: 'Do you want a drink?' I thought, I'll have a morsel of fun, so I talked in a Cockney accent. Got a cider. I flashed my smile in gratitude. Switch on. Switch off. Results. More ciders followed. Cockney continued. About reality and all that shit. He just couldn't figure me out. He was confused to despairing point. Told him I came from Portsmouth and that my name was Syd. He shouted across to his friends, 'God — you try and talk to her, I'm too confused. I don't know what's happening at all.'

His other two friends went off to the Victoria and left me to confuse the third. He said, 'Can I sit down?' So he sat next to me. I later learned his name was Eddie. Brown straight hair. Brown eyes, bags under eyes. But nice.

'You've got a beautiful profile,' he says to me.

'Don't be funny,' I said. Sarcasm lowest form of wit, etc.

'No, honestly you have,' he said. He was so frank.

'Why did you buy me a drink?' I asked.

''Cos I fancied you!' he said.

82

He made me laugh, he was so nice and funny. He went on about his ultimate trip at the Isle of Wight pop festival last year. We talked about all the ghastly people in the Bowling Green. He put his arm round my shoulders, which was nice. He said, 'It's so different meeting a bird who's more intelligent than yourself' (oneself). Then he said, 'Eh, you're talkin' great now — I really dig you, you know.' The 'dig' wasn't repulsive, so it was OK.

He asked if he could walk me home. I agreed. I could tell he was mad about me already so I knew that he'd ask to see me again. But I couldn't becos of Trev. So decided to say that I was gay.

'I hope you realise I'm gay,' I said suddenly.

He stopped abruptly by the bus shelter. 'Yer what?'

'I'm gay,' I said.

'Oh, Jesus,' he said, 'you can't be! Look at you, yer beautiful! Oh, Jesus, you can't be!' He grabbed hold of me and ran his hands up and down my arms in sheer desperation. I didn't realise it would affect him so greatly. He said, 'Well, all I can say is you're wasted — you could have loads of guys!'

Then he said, 'Look, does it offend you holding my hand!'

'No, it doesn't bother me really,' I said.

He said, 'I meet a bird who I really dig, a bird who I really fancy, and look what happens!'

God, I felt rotten. I'd taken the bottom out of his world with a bang. Christ, I hadn't realised how he'd feel. He said, 'Do you mind if I kiss you?'

After he'd kissed me I clung to him and said, 'You make me feel normal for a while.'

He said, kissing me, 'God bless your eyes, God bless your nose, God bless your lips and God bless everything you have.' He kissed me frantically then and said, 'God, I'll love you for ever.' He said he'd come and talk to me if I was ever in the Bowling Green.

I couldn't get over how really nice he was. The way he

talked to me, it was like in a movie but without the corn. It was fantastic. He was so nice. He said suddenly, 'God, you're a bitch, aren't you? You're a bitch to me, anyway. Shut up. You'll have me in tears in a minute.' Christ, how I must have hurt him. He said desperately, 'I can't leave you!'

I said, 'You must!' And so we parted. But my God I want to see him again. Physically, mostly, I think. To have someone hug me! My life at present is so lopsided. Nobody has ever said things that he said to me tonight. The level of intellect disturbs me, though.

Saturday, 10th July

Got up feeling vomitable. Three and a half pints of cider. God, I felt rotten. Went to see Tina and Jacko in the Robin Hood before meeting Trev. Eddie came in. I brushed past him and said, 'Hello.' He smiled and said, 'Hiyah.' Later he left. My heart sank. Was that all I had to say to him after last night? God, I'm insensitive at times!

Went to meet Trev in the Wimpy. Felt moody. Went in the sunken gardens. He said, 'Are you going to tell me what's up?' I didn't answer. Later I said, 'I'd rather not be with you tonight.' I needed to see Eddie. I needed him. Went looking. Robin Hood, Flying Horse, Bowling Green, Victoria, Jolly Waggoner, searching hopelessly. Heart lumpy. Sinking. Drowning. Why couldn't I find him? Home at about 10.30. Abandonment. Must see him. Wonder why he didn't say anything to me, why he left so soon after. Had he seen through my thin veneer? Christ, where is he?

Sunday, 11th July

I have nothing, absolutely nothing to look forward to. *Romeo and Juliet* I am dreading. Upper Sixth—God, the work that must come! Told Nancy of my lies about being gay. She was appalled. She said it was the cruellest thing I could have done to anyone and to myself. She was horrified. She made me realise just how many lies I'd been telling and how many acts I put on. She told me that I'd better stop acting. I said that it didn't really bother me if people thought I was gay.

Heard from Tina that Jud did not turn up on Friday because he thought I wouldn't come. I think I believe that. She said he was really agitated and annoyed and kicking himself for not turning up. I'm known amongst Jacko's friends as Tina's Mad Mate Margaret.

Wednesday, 14th July

Morag woke up in the middle of the night screaming and I found myself standing over her clutching her hand—she only reminded me of it just now. I'd completely forgotten, but, Christ, she scared me. Miro has arrived with a glass crystal intricate ball and steel wine goblet for Morag.

Thursday, 15th July

Morag and Miro set off for Ireland plus rucksacks, etc.

Friday, 16th July

Went to Stratford in a minibus with Workshop. Pregnant lady sat next to me. Read 59 pages of *The Age of Reason* (Jean Paul Sartre)—begun as an excuse for not talking but became interesting. Went in rowing boat on the river. I rowed. It was really funny, almost hysterical. Horrible feeling of being a 'tourist'—yeuk! Wanted to be a traveller with a rucksack passing through and hitching lifts. Saw some hitchhikers and made me want to hitch it to London in August. Judi Dench was the Duchess of Malfi: fantastic surprise. Julia Moran and Gerard slobbering over each other all the time — very sickly. Julia Moran wimpers pseudo delicately, plays the English Rose type and gets away with it. Fake, fake! Listen who's talking! Some ignorant stupid idiot said on the bus back that they didn't like J. Dench's voice and that the serving maid had a nicer voice than hers. Gawd, what the hell has niceness got to do with it?

Saturday, 17th July

Have decided definitely to hitch down to London instead of catching the coach — more fun, more excitement, less boring. Saw Trev last night. He was in an extremely happy mood. Said he'd had ten pints last night. Went in Coach and Horses and saw Liam McNair with the girl who works behind the bar of the Bowling Green. Went to Castle and stayed there. Aunty Lil and Uncle Boris were there again. God, I hope I don't take after my relations. Trev said me and Tina can stay overnight at his flat in London, so that's good. He said he's going to save up for a motorbike. Wonder if he'll change at all during his year in London.

Sunday, 18th July

Dave came to tea. It was awful. Introductions, embarrassing, socialising unbearable, didn't talk. Went to Workshop where the Improvisation Course was in progress. Couldn't join in, don't know why, made me think about my ability to be an actress or even a teacher — of anything. Frightening. Felt as if I was slipping quietly out of the back door of a party, felt inadequate. Made me weep to see Nancy walking up the road talking to, looking at, Dave. I felt as though she was going further and further away from me. Dave is the all-important one now. I just fill in the time when she's not with Dave. It now feels as though we are two girlfriends catching up on all the goings on and gossip, it's horrid.

Monday, 19th July

Dear Lord, give me a friend!

Tuesday, 20th July

No school. Stayed at home with Nancy, talked together for first time in ages. Good, nice, near, true. Wept hopelessly last night at the thought of rejections from Drama Schools and Universities — too much, too big, too high, too hopeless. Nancy told me today that she would love, more than anything else, to live on a farm and be a farmer's wife and write novels during the day. Novelty would wear off after a bit, though, wouldn't it?

Read some John Donne poems today. Surprisingly liked them. Talks about how his heart has been shattered into pieces on account of his first love so

> My ragges of heart can wish, like and adore
> But after one such love, can love no more.
>
> 'Tis true 'tis day; what though it be?
> O wilt thou therefore rise from me?
> Why should we rise, because 'tis light?
> Did we lie downe, because 'twas night?

Went to Workshop at night, but no rehearsal for me so went round to Tina's. Tina was out and her mum answered the door with her cheeks wet with tears. She brought me in and started asking me about Jacko. Someone had told her that Jacko was a drug addict. She'd been crying all afternoon about it. Went on about how scruffy he was, how Tina had changed, how if people saw young girls coming in at midnight, that young girl got a bad reputation, etc. So exaggerated. Could understand how she felt, though — God, that sounds patronising. Reassured her as best I could.

Mr Lubicz was marvellous, he had the right idea. Said that clothes did not reflect a person's true personality or character. Said, 'Look at students: they wear scruffy jeans and long hair but they have brilliant minds, they're not stupid.' Said, 'Hippies are fighting for freedom just like we fought for freedom during the War, so we must not be disgusted with the hippies, we should admire them just as people admired the soldiers.' Said, 'We've had our fun, now let Tina have her fun. If Jacko had only wanted sex, etc., the relationship would not have lasted so long. So it must be good and all right.'

Have decided (out of fear mostly) to take a tent and stay on a campsite so we'll be safer and it'll be cheaper than youth hostelling. Must ask Tina + Deirdre what they think.

Thursday, 22nd July

Dad told me today that he didn't like the idea of me going camping with two girls. Bluddy 'ell, I really fancied the idea. Nancy doesn't think he'll let me go.

Mum started tonight. 'Have you no homework to do? You don't seem to be doing any work these days. We've been told by reports over the phone from teachers that your attitude to work isn't good enough and you don't seem to be mixing in with the other girls at school, we don't hear about you having any friends at school. Why have you dropped Karen?' etc.

My God! I couldn't bear it. If only she knew. Everybody at school in pairs — everybody having a best friend; tears poured, couldn't stop. I always have people around me or I am always around other people, but I have no special friend, no one to wait for me at 4.15. Everybody is paired off. It didn't use to be like this for me, I always used to have a best friend. What's happened? I'm conscious of being on my own every time I walk across town. I feel as though everybody knows I'm on my own with no friend. I've been dead a long, long time. Who cares? Listening Stones LP *High Tide and Green Grass*.

Couldn't tell Trev about what Mum said about friends. Nobody except Nancy. But not even Nancy really, 'cos although I'm her friend and I love her, I don't think the love is as great on her side. We are not equal, on the same level, that is why. I'm younger, not as intelligent, and also she is big sister; so even though we are very friendly she'll never look up to me as a great friend, never. Why should she? She's got Dave. And she's got Sharon Wilton who cried at having to leave Nancy in England while she went off to Austria to do V.S.O. Who the bluddy 'ell have I got? Tessa, but then I'm only a third party. I tag along and entertain, but I come second on the list if either Tessa or Helen wants somebody to go into town with them. And then with Nancy I'm only fourth party. Nancy first, Dave second, Sharon third, me fourth.

God, imagine making such a bloody list! Christ! I want shooting! And then after all this I've got to go and do *Romeo and Juliet*.

Friday, 23rd July

Went to see Trev in Wimpy. Felt surprisingly good and all right. Went to Seven Stars, came out straight away. Awful. Went in a pub then came back into Rochdale and went to Castle. Vincent Roache in the same room. Played Greta Garbo type. Controller woman. Countless expressions to suggest distance, remoteness, dominance, etc. Vincent was intrigued. Never looked him in the eye. Did not give him any of my attention. He wanted it desperately. Trev couldn't understand what I was doing. Thought something was wrong. Kept asking, 'What's up? What's the matter?' etc. Kept calling me love. Trev said he's found a word to describe me — supersensitive. It pleased me somewhat. He's going to London in two weeks' time.

Saturday, 24th July

Thunder and lightning violently last night. Nancy jumped out of bed and grabbed hold of me and we went along to Mum and Dad's bedroom, terrified like in the War, all the family, split-second reunion. It was beautiful when Nancy came to me and grabbed me and said, 'Oh, Margaret, are you all right?' Protection. She really must care for me. SHE LOVES ME!

Went to Workshop at 2.00 afternoon. Talk on mask work in the theatre. Boring after a bit, went on for too long. At first it was really marvellous. Miro and Morag have come back from Ireland. Morag has a ring on her wedding finger!?! Intrigue!

I think it's only a curtain ring and means nothing. Sullivan is always saying that in the theatre if a designer takes away the fourth wall of a room he takes away the reality. But is there any reality in theatre?

Wednesday, 28th July

Fear is amplified second by second about *Romeo and Juliet*.

Less than a fortnight to go. Lines are not learned. Nicholas cross-eyed Fletcher is horrible bossy and patronising and takes people aside after rehearsals to give them advice! The living of Juliet seems nearer to me now. Have a terrible cold, exactly same as the one I had for *Pirates of Penzance*.

Went to see Trev at night. He was peculiar. He just said, 'I'll see yer, then,' and closed the door immediately. Got prospectus from Bristol Univ.

Think will apply there for English and Drama. Must write to Birmingham.

Have now broken up for the holidays. We go away soon! Must go and see Tina! + Deirdre.

Saturday, 31st July

Another month of my youth has gone by. Nancy told me last night that she thinks she and Dave have finished. She told me of how emotional and neurotic he is. He walked out of the Spread Eagle when she went to the toilet — when she came back he'd gone. So she followed him. Then he went to his bus stop and she went to hers. It's all to do with the fact that she can't see him this weekend because of rehearsals. He said to her that she should not tolerate all his sulks and moods and that it wasn't fair to her being treated like that, and that she should finish with him. But surely, if sulks and moods can finish a relationship the relationship must not have been worth anything in the first place. Now she lies on her bed and goes into the front room listening to records, and hardly speaks. God, I hope they're not finished.

Thoughts about my future clash and confuse. No idea. Scared. Disillusioned. Am wondering about Trev. Don't know what to do. Hope I see him before he goes. My cold has made me deaf, horrible.

August

Your Stars for August

If you're feeling stretched in too many directions all at once, you may need extra reassurance this month from those closest to you. But whatever pressures you're under, try and be sensitive to the needs of friends both male and female. If it all gets too much, an adventure holiday could be just the thing to help you relax and be yourself.

Tuesday, 3rd August

Mum and Dad's 25th wedding anniversary. We all had to go to Mass. Mum and Dad knelt on kneelers at the front. Aunty Jessie cried. The lovely serene nuns sang, on whispered request, Dad's favourite psalm: 'The Lord's My Shepherd'. Went afterwards to the Norden Chimney for a meal. Aunty Barbara miles away, neurotic stares all through the meal. Uncle Paul ghostlike, quiet, but Daniel did the honourable/charming thing and started chatting to him. Aunty Eileen highly intelligent and witty. Uncle Derek treats women as though they are stupid and thick. Aunty Eileen talks non-stop about her kids.

Dad gave Mum her present. We were all dying to know what it was. Mum, surrounded by all, opened the present (it was like a photograph of a bride showing her ring to her bridesmaids). It was a beautiful silver bracelet. Exquisite. Mum wore it. She's very bonny. Mum and Dad got lots of cards, which was nice.

Thursday, 5th August

Well, here I am here hear ear EARS! I can hear perfectly. Went to the doctors. Lovely smiling Doctor Wiggins syringed my ears and pulled a dirty great brown lump out. Amplified microphones megaphones central station aeroplanes terrifying fantastic soles clicked along pavement key rattled in the door car droned heavily clock ticking legs of jeans rubbing together. Crikey!

I have not altogether steered clear of Rochdale Arts Festival. Late night pop concerts nightly ten till midnight. All the youth of Rochdale — greasers, skins, weirds, mods, the lot.

It's all okay with Nancy and Dave now, I think. I haven't seen Tina for weeks. Must. Don't know what it's all about with Trev. Wonder if I'll ever hear from him again! Nancy is brilliant on stage. Sullivan never says anything about me or to me when we're rehearsing at night. I wish he would. My lines are all learned. I can now only hope! I feel so utterly alone!

Friday, 6th August

Letter from Trev. Peculiar, all formal all humble, pedestal bit again: couldn't bear it. He asked me to meet him on Saturday in the Coach and Horses, but I can't possibly be there until about 10 at the very earliest. He'll be going to London next week.

Mum in vile mood today. Dad went to the doctors about his back. My God, the heaves and the sighs and the pants, you'd think he'd had his leg amputated.

Tuesday, 10th August

Dress rehearsal went quite well. More concentration, but even more needed. Wish I could have a pair of blinkers so I would not see the audience. Finished at about half four and walked into town with Arnold Cunningham. He looks a lot older than he is. He hasn't even done his 'O' levels yet. Looks about 17 easily. Pseudo tendencies, I suspect. He's quite ugly really — listen who's talking! Got my school report today through the post. I suppose it was an all right one. But, Christ, they act as if they knew me!

Isle of Wight festival is off! FUCK! KCUF!

Wednesday, 11th August

First performance of *R & Juliet* to which Mr Diggle came. I was coming out of the toilets and into the makeup and changing room when he grabbed me and said, 'Hey, come here.' He gave me a big hug and said, 'I'm proud of you. Super! Are you pleased?'

I said, 'No, not really,' and he embraced me once more and said, 'Of course you are.' Sullivan didn't say much except that 'there were all sorts of golden opinions about it, as Macbeth would say.' I wonder if Diggle really meant what he said. I wish I could be sure. Nancy told me after that Sullivan told her about a teacher saying during the interval, 'I must go and congratulate Juliet after the play.'

Saturday, 14th August

Last performance of *Rom & Jul*. Vile becos of Mum and Dad's presence. Party after. Sullivan talked to me all night until his girlfriend came and took him off. Everybody re-voltingly paired off. I refused offers from Arnold to dance. I wanted solitariness. The whole thing made me cry, I was so alone. Nancy let herself go with Barry the Friar. She got drunk and threw up in the corridor.

Sullivan said to me that I was ready to go to drama school now. But he said I wasn't ready to play Lady Macbeth yet 'cos I'd never lived away from home. He said he'd love to see me do a really big part. He said, 'Ophelia's too easy.' He said, 'Come back here after two years at drama school and I want to see you play Desdemona!'

Thursday, 19th August

Youth hostel, Windsor. The German boy (who stared at me intently outside when we were waiting for the hostel to open) came and sat next to me in the common room. We played cards, then went to the pub down the road. German boy came and Deirdre, and a nothingness boy came too. Ended up in a beer Keller in town centre. Raining when we got outside. Walked a little then decided to run. After a while we all joined hands and ran in the rain.

Pause for breath and the pause separated us into pairs.

German boy kept hold of my hand strongly, which was nice and secretive. Gradually we walked along with our arms round each other. It was sort of understood that I'd let him and that he'd let me. He put his hand on and around my head, which was nice. The other two went into the hostel but he dragged me back and began kissing me all over. Taste of orange because he'd just had a quick orange in a pub we'd been in to shelter from the rain. We stood in the garden of the youth hostel and kissed and touched and felt. He was taller than me and so he kept lifting me up so that our frontal parts could make contact and sensation. He went to my dormitory door with me and we kissed on the corridor. Everything was shallow and superficial but I didn't care. I was tired of everything.

Deirdre was in bed when I got into the dormitory. In a stupid way I felt superior to all the other girls already in bed. I felt wanted. Why shouldn't I kid myself? I felt good, only the glow of goodness was lukewarm and easily extinguishable. God, I sound like a pseudo trying to write. Which is what I am. So who cares? I do!

Friday, 20th August

Met German boy again at breakfast. He followed me around annoyingly. But they (he and his sister and her fella) gave us a lift to London, so who's complaining? Hands almost touched in the car. Eyes touched. They dropped us off at London Trafalgar Square and he kissed me as I got out the car. End of that little episode of nothingness.

Monday, 23rd August

Trev's bedsit. Deirdre decided out of boredom and lack of money to go home. Trev told me his 'A' level results: one A, three Bs and a D. I couldn't get over it. I was so excited, so happy, so pleased. It's bloody marvellous. He went off to work and I went down Tottenham Court Rd and halfway along Oxford Street. Went to Nat. Youth Theatre and got a book on it which is pretty useless. Helen Mirren went to New College. Went to see RADA and got a prospectus. Saw Hare Krishna going along street chanting. Young blond Cockney lad (listen to grandma here) chatted me up and offered to let me sleep at his flat. Lied to him like hell. Told him I'd been on the road for six months and felt like Jools Driscoll. Pseudo!!!!!

Stayed up talking to Trev at night. Dreamed about Nancy and Dave's 'A' level results. Horrible dream. It's going to be difficult writing letters to Trev. People are peculiar beings in letters. They become the words the letters the sentences the commas the exclamations, etc., and nothing else.

Tuesday, 24th August

I'm hooked on Yoghurt! It's terrific, or super as Sullivan would say. Went to library at St. Pancras. Boy kept smiling at me and we laughed silently at all the peculiar people in the library. God, it sounds like a story out of *Petticoat*! Bluddy 'ell. Read *The Entertainer* and enjoyed it. Bloody good!

Went to coach station after to meet Tina. She got off the coach followed by Jacko. Didn't explain Jacko's presence. She tried to smooth it over by saying, 'Oh, I *am* tired,' and bits of nothings like that, so I said, 'What are you doing now, then?' (knowing that she would be coming with me to Trev's), but she said, 'We're going to Whitechapel, to Ben and Stan's flat.' So I said, 'What are you doing next week?' She said, 'Oh yeah, we're going to Clacton to the festival.'

I felt ignored. I felt idiotic. There was no room for me in their plans. She had apparently abandoned our plan of going on holiday together. She pretended she'd forgotten. The bleedin-rotten bitch, I could have kicked her. There she was acting as if everything was okay. However, I was quite glad really, 'cos it meant I didn't have to go on holiday again. So I made a nonchalant departure and a rather superior departure, saying, 'I'll see yer, then,' and walked off down the road back to the library. I remembered then that I'd paid her bloody coach fare down to London. She owes me £1.60 and I'm going to get it. I felt glad I could go home, though.

Wednesday, 25th August

Arrived home, no one in. Morag and Nancy came in at about 6 pm. Morag's hair was cropped really short. Nancy quiet, peculiar mood. Sensed something was wrong. She told me she'd got a B–English, C–Sociology, and D–French. Didn't seem very pleased. Then she told me, 'We finished last night.' Thud. Tears. Incredulous. My God. And then Morag tells me, 'Don't ask Nancy about Dave yet.' The bloody nerve, as if I would. Horror. Couldn't believe it. I'd seen a candle and candlestick in blue and grey on our dressing table and almost cried because their love was so overwhelming to me. And now it's finished. It can't be, though.

I asked her later what had happened but she didn't say. I wasn't there. Morag was there, and I felt like an outsider, a bloody visitor, an intruder. Felt so out of touch. I wish to God I'd been there. It's made a gap between us somehow. God, I hope they're not finished for good. I hope with all my might that he'll phone her or something.

Miro rang Morag at night. Unbearable, I'm surprised Nancy didn't walk out. I hope Dave won't be proud and stupid and not phone her. Please, dear God, bring them together again. She loves him. He loves her. Oh please, dear God, I beg you.

Tina phoned late. She was in Whitechapel. She couldn't understand why I'd gone home. She asked whether I was coming down again or not! Bloody cheek!

Thursday, 26th August

The day is Thursday and the mood is black. The day drags and it's still Thursday. Morag told me she was woken up on Tuesday night by the sound of Nancy in tears. Apparently Nancy and Dave had been for a drink with some of his friends and Dave had said that there was something missing. Nancy lay on her bed weeping and told Morag it was all over. Tears pricked my eyes. Try and control them. God, I can't believe it. He walked out of this house on Tuesday night and out of her life. Christ! I don't understand. It can't just finish like that. Oh please, dearest God, let them be re-united, please! Every time the phone rings or someone knocks, my heart leaps in hope that it will be Dave. Oh please — don't be proud! We hardly speak. Except when she asked me about my holiday but avoided and ignored her parting from Dave. God, I wish we could speak. I wish I'd never gone away. To hell with bloody holidays. It's done a great deal of irreparable damage. The gap between us is widening. Soon I'll no longer be a peninsular — I'll be an island.

I realise that all I am is hers. My thoughts used to be hers. My likes and dislikes are hers. My acting is based on her ways. My exam answers are hers. My ideas are hers. Everything I have, is or used to be hers. I have nothing. I am not me. I am a mirror, a shadow, a piece of carbon paper. My behaviour in a crowd (say at a party) is a copy of Garbo's. My relationship with Trev — I try to make it like I think Keith Franklin and Rosie's was. Nothing is me. Nothing original. I am no creator. If I am, the products are merely pieces of carbon paper. Always bloody copying. I am other people. Sheep. Stupid sheep! When the mirror gets dusty and I can see through it no more, only then will I be happy. Only then will I be able to create, to make something that is MINE. Christ, I don't know the meaning of the bloody word!

Friday, 27th August

Nancy came up to the bedroom and I asked her what she was going to do about Dave. She asked me, 'What *should* I do?' We talked at last. I helped a little, I think. Suggested that he might be thinking it was her who wanted to finish and so he wouldn't phone for fear of rejection. So she decided to phone him. She went. Resolved. Fear. Utterness. Faint hope. Fear of her return.

She came back breathless and running up the stairs. 'You were right.' Thank God, it was all right. Thank you, dear God. We shook with ecstatic joy and relief. It was fantastic. We talked and ran downstairs to tell Morag. The gap disappeared gradually, then instantly. She'd thought that I'd feel out of things and ignored but she was too upset to talk and tell all. But now — glorious. The blister has healed. She showed me a picture of Sharon Wilton smiling at her 'intended'. God, it's so good. So bloody good. I live again.

Saturday, 28th August

Sunny Saturday. Read *The Observer* and found to my great surprise that I'd passed General Studies. Got a rise at work to £1.25, which was another surprise. Went to meet Trev in Castle. Bad. Headache. Stupid. Had to sit there at an appointed time and had to talk between 9 pm and half 11. Ridiculous. I was bad company. He seemed exceptionally happy. Went home on the bus at 10 o'clock. I'm a bitch, a selfish bitch. I've mucked up his weekend, right good and proper.

Sunday, 29th August

To you and only you

Christ, this is terrible! I've sat here for the past half hour not knowing how or where to start. I hate writing bloody letters. However, being, as we all know, a kind-hearted and considerate wench, I will continue. I should think that Dylan is exhausted by now, having gone round the turntable God knows how many times in the past few hours. Morag goes to Austria on 23rd September — just thought I might tell you.

And now the weather . . .

Think I'll go and see *The Music Lovers* sometime. Me mum and dad and Nancy have seen it. Nancy said it's sensational, horrific, badly put together, but the music terrific.

Me mum's just brought me in a cup of tea and gave me a knowing look. Teenage moods, no doubt, I don't know. Thought you'd be pleased to know that I vomited when I got in last night. My head was pounding away right up till this afternoon, thank you very much. Apology **accepted**. Interval.

Have just seen *Green Julia* on telly. Bloody good! Goody blood! Feel bloated. I hope you follow the advice, my dear, that I gave you last night: that of talking to people. I don't mean starting interesting or pleasant conversations during coffee but just don't shut yourself off completely because, as I said, you get a little bit of something from everybody. Marje Proops has nothing on me. I feel very ugly. Think I'll start reading books, so then I'll have something interesting to talk or write about.

Everybody has gone to bed. The telly's off and it's raining. Read an Ezra Pound gem last night. Requiescat in pace!

What a bitty letter! Hope you realise that the only reason I'm struggling to write this letter is that I love getting letters and saving them to read at dinnertime or anytime. You must admit I'm subtle with me hints. Christ, that was terrible! — I repeat myself merely to cover up writing space.

Bloody 'ell ↑

Live for today 'cos tomorrow won't come, so they say.

People sound horrid through letters, completely different. This is not me, is it? But how would *you* know? Apologies, ajopolies.

When you want to die you're dead, so keep hoping/crying/sighing/praying/smiling.

R.S.V.P.

Margaret

The need to be neutral

September

Your Stars for September

Aims and ambitions are very much to the fore this month, so you'll need lots of energy at work if things are to run smoothly for you. If you know your limitations and can allow for flexibility you won't go far wrong. Someone you thought you could trust may upset you this month; if so, try and see it as a challenge rather than a tragedy.

Dear Margaret,

This is the fifth try. And the last. The trouble is, you see, I don't know what to put. If I knew what to put I would just put it and that would be one end to the matter. I've just read the letter you wrote to me. I could not understand some of it. Bloody Yelloways were full so I went on North Western, which only takes four hours.

Writing letters is different from spoken forms of communication and should be considered differently, or should I say separately, since the whole of the mind during the period of letter writing is working towards a written end. It ought to be possible to write what you would say, but it is not. Enough.

Coffee breaks, or tea breaks as I call them, have got worse since they now play darts instead of cards, and a middle-aged woman with a loud voice — speaks broad Cockney — has joined us after three weeks' holiday in Scotland, and for an hour a day I can hear all about her and her life. She remembers what the weather was like on any day in the past six months or so. I got my wages — £27.75. You don't get a bank book, you get a cheque book.

I have not smoked since I returned to the City in which I am and the beginnings of my paragraphs are arbitrary or random, both or neither or either one, each none or all.

This letter and any more I may write will look bad in the appendix of my autobiography. The first 17 years of which I wrote on the back of my tube ticket this morning. That, of course, is a joke, but it is not funny, unlike some jokes.

I can count the number of letters I have written on the fingers of one hand, so I am no good at them, though I think I will improve. The first one was definitely worse than this.

> Sir, more than kisses, letters mingle souls;
> For, thus friends absent speak.

The next letter I write I won't use the word 'letter'.

It's all very silly.

Someone just rang my bell. It was a pools collector.

I was interested to learn that you had the intensely exciting experience of vomiting. The worst bit is about two seconds before you start, when you resign yourself to spewing and just hope for time to pass! Isn't it?

At this point I read your letter again.

I hope you don't say you feel very ugly to cue me to contradict it, but you probably don't.

I used a computer today.

> Love is like a mutton chop,
> Sometimes cold and sometimes hot.
>
> —my Gran

I can't think of very much more to put. I've put quite a lot already. I've put all I can and I can't put no more. I look forward to seeing what you'll put in your next letter.

I am coming home on the 18th — not to see *Macbeth* — though I may see *Macbeth* for a muffled laugh.

So foul and fair a play I have not seen.

My letter is finished and I am reasonably pleased with it and have unexpectedly enjoyed writing it.

I hope you'll write very soon.

If not very soon then fairly soon
> or quite soon
> or just soon.

Has 'soon' got an opposite?
> Enough.

Hoping to hear from you soon.

Trevor Saunders

(Most people who call me anything call me Trev, by the way.)

*For 'Dylan' in your letter may I read 'Bob Dylan'?

I liked/enjoyed your letter.
> Enough.

105

To nobody in particular, but you will do as well as anybody

I've just received a letter from the Oldham and District Organists' and Choirmasters' Association. Excuse me, dear, could you please tell me when your next sermon will be?

Boring golden oldies! Christ! No? No! No! No!

And now the letter.

What 'putty' letters you write. (It occurred eight times!) Was that the idea? There will be ten people sleeping at our house this weekend — two friends of Morag from college + Miro (her intended) + all us lot. Me dad's in the bath. I hope that bit about you taking your cue was meant to be a joke. If not, what the bloody 'ell do you take me for?

Macbeth starts on Sat 11 Sept–Wed 15 Sept. So I'm told. Saw Matthew Wallis on the bus yesterday, so he must be alive and kicking yet again. I love lavatories!

Seem to visit Dylan (yes, Dylan!) every half hour these days.

My subtle hints almost match up to your subtle and nasty digs. Which you managed to make every ten words or so all the way through your letter. I must keep trying.

Got a letter from the Dept (ugh!) of Health and Social Security yesterday, all about National Insurance cards. Most peculiar, didn't understand a word. I'm hungry! For everything.

The desire to be undesirable is my core.

The woman across the road is a younger version of Annie Walker. I don't even know her name. It's horrid here. When we lived in Kensington Street we knew everybody and everybody knew us, i.e. everybody knew everybody else's business. But here there's a dirty great big road preventing us from knowing the second Annie Walker's business. Pity.

Ignore the above nauseating nostalgia, if you please. You will by now have gathered that I am totally incapable of writing a letter, because, admit it, this is not a proper letter, is it? Abominable creature that I am. Lonely hours, lonely days, where am I going without Nancy? I love her! Is that really so hard to believe? Life is for learning, life is for loving, life is for living. Christ! I sound like bloody Donovan!

Hope everything is just all right.

Margaret

Monday, 6th September

In letters people are masked and lost behind fashionable methods of writing and so letters merely succeed in defeating their own object (i.e. communication). Winter is approaching me. I'm so glad. It's dark and cold in bed. Hot water bottles make me safe. My tears prick me. I want to give in but can't. Oh God, give me a friend, imagination, a place, a hope, a chance, something. I am alone, I feel so utterly singular. Nobody cares about how I am or where I am or whether I go out or whether. Nobody comes and calls for me, nobody comes to see me, nobody comes to talk to me, nobody asks me to go out with them. The above nobodys are girls. I love Nancy but she doesn't love me half as much as I love her. She doesn't need me. She doesn't need to see me. She doesn't need to talk to me. I'm at the bottom of an enormous mountain and I doubt if I'll ever reach the top. It's too huge, too far away, too hopeless; drama school is only about 100 feet up, it's not anywhere near the top. I will say again I look around and I've lost my friends. That was years ago, I should have gotten used to it by now. We begin to be 'friends' again on the first day of term and cease to be 'friends' on the last day of term.

I knew a nun once who disagreed altogether with the idea of diaries: 'The past is meant to be forgotten, that's why we have past, present and future,' she said. She was going to be a doctor, but when she entered the convent and became a nun they needed a music teacher for their school and so she had to give up her medical training which she loved and had to start training as a music teacher. But to look at her and listen to her you would think that she had been dedicated to music since she was born and that she had always wanted to be a music teacher; she had hidden her real ambition away from us and pretended for the sake of her faith that she loved teaching music. Isn't 'admire' a weak word? She makes me feel ashamed, selfish, shallow and guilty.

Wednesday, 8th September

Going to see *Measure for Measure* at Victoria Theatre, Stoke-on-Trent, in November, which should be bloody awful; I sincerely hope it comes up to expectations. I realise more and more that I write not in ecstasy or depression but in the memory of it. I ashamed, have completed the act of prying into Nancy's diary. I now realise I don't mean anything to her. Sheer circumstance and conventional reasons explain our rapport. I thought she at least was my friend. She is a mere sister. No, I'm a mere sister to her. But who'd want a nosey, inquisitive cheat for a friend, anyway? I figure hardly at all in her writings. If she ever found out I'd read her diary she would quite rightly never speak to me again. God, I'm a leech. Trevor has not written. I fear my letter was too harsh/false/offhand.

Dear Margaret,
    Thanks muchly (dear me) for your recentmost letter. You forgot to tell me to respond but I have done — I hope you don't mind. I read it this morning and spent the whole day formulating this reply, though this is not what I formu-

lated, and decided to use the words 'alive and kicking' to express my thoughts about one M. Wallis's recovery from his testicular complaint. I've just got back and seen that you used the words, so I cannot now do so. This will be long and boring, but consider, please, my situation.

So I won't see *Macbeth* after all. Ah well. If you see it on Saturday write me about it and specially 1) the witches, 2) Jim Dudley's head at the end.

Sorry about unintended digs. The Dylan one was intended but only as good clean fun.

I'm suffering very nicely at the moment. Really down, as I like to be. Consequently this letter may not be as funny as I thought my last (or indeed first) one was. I expected praise or something.

I've been granted £45 a year for my 'A' levels. The letter said 'in recognition of your three "A" level passes'. I wonder why they said three. The grant is given for two—perhaps there has been a mistake.

I got an electric shock today and involuntarily shouted, 'Fuck!' at the top of my voice, and ''in 'ell' in a whisper as I became conscious I was being obscene. The blood group lady looked disgusted.

Today I had a lengthy discussion with two people about H.J. Eysenck (you know, the professor who says blacks are intrinsically thicker than whites). It was not a tea break, however; those are still hell.

I am reading Jung's psychology, so prepare to be bored when I see you next time. It's really good.

That 'put' was meant to have you rolling about in an uncontrollable fit of laughter, but it didn't. Did you laugh at any of my jokes?

Memphis Slim is giving two concerts in London on 1st October. I am really excited. Thrilled, in fact, to bits.

Before you listen to much (you win again) Dylan, consider that I have spent much of my time these past six to twelve months listening to his renderings. If that doesn't put you off nought will.

I thought of copying out one of Keats' letters to Fanny Brawne when he was in Italy, but you wouldn't swallow it.

I laughed the other day when I heard a British soldier in Ulster had defected to the IRA. That *is* funny.

I'm fucking useless at money. I got paid on Tuesday and already I've worked out that I've got 40p a day till I get paid again. Deary me. Dreary me.

I hope you did intend to write again. Yes, you did.

This letter is not funny so I'll tell a joke:

A: Why do farts smell?

B: I don't know why.

A: For the benefit of the deaf.

School again on Tuesday. Ah, well! Never mind.

I'm going home on 18th, Saturday. If you've no obs., tell me where you'll be at half past eight and I'll be there.

I've eaten nowt today, and when I seal/ceil/seel this rag up I'll cook a tin of spaghetti I've just bought for 7p. I've got a pan.

Either it'll get better or I'll get used to it.

Yellow bloody Pages is on next door's telly. It's about quarter to seven.

Write soon, please

Yours marginally (pun)

   Trevor Saunders

Say bye bye to the children, Sooty.

'Bye bye, everyone.'

  Bye Bye

   See yer

I think this letter is fairly me.

Friday, 10th September

Trevor wrote and made me laugh. Had silly doubts about a pregnancy — German boy. Completely unfounded, thank God. I'm sure Trev's brother doesn't think I'm worthy of

110

going around with Trevor. He probably thinks Trev's just infatuated with a pretty face. Pretty? Ye Gods!

Monday, 13th September

Went to Theatre Workshop to look at photos of *R. & Juliet* in colour. Only Sullivan there. Stayed for three hours talking to him. It was good. Told him so many things. Let out many secrets of mine. He still doesn't know me. He thinks he does. I didn't tell him, but I've decided to go to University if I get a place at both University and Drama School. 'Cos from a Drama degree you can go into the theatre and it also will give me something to fall back on if I get nowhere in acting. Think I'd tell Sullivan that Dad made me take the Univ place, which he would. I think it's best. Hope I get a place.

Tuesday, 14th September

First crowded jam-packed day at school. Uppity Sixth. Lots to say. Like all other first days back, it was good, exciting. Tessa and Helen are my main 'friends', I think. Didn't speak to M. Fisher at all. Need to impress Lower Sixth — somehow. *Sons and Lovers* is involving.

Went to Eye Clinic. Showed off, amused and entertained L. Wisdish and Tina. Don't need glasses. Put drops in my eyes and made my pupils go bigger. Look like black holes of oil. Reading was blurred. Nancy's glasses helped. They are now back to normal size. I looked as if I was stoned or something. I'm worried about my possible stagnation.

Wednesday, 15th September

Last night I wished I was a boy so that I might have a chance of having and keeping with Nancy.
She goes away soon.
Too soon.

When I see girls walking along the street together I think: it's not fair, they will be split up when any boys come along. One girl will go to one boy and the other girl will go to another. Divided, inevitable. Have written for application forms to various acting schools. Want to go to University, though. Only eight and a half months to get two Bs in! Morag saw the doctor today. She's got a cyst in the ovaries and has to go into hospital. She wept. Her Austria trip will have to be put off till later. Horrible. Please, God, let her be all right!

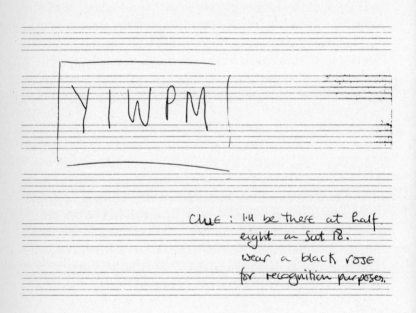

Friday, 17th September

Scared out of my wits about 'A' levels. Possibilities of getting good grades and into University decrease minute by minute. God only knows how I'll get my Latin. Please, dear God, help me to concentrate and remember things and help me to get the good grades I need for Univ. Please!!!! I talk to Tessa more and more. I hope it lasts. I reckon Karen's in love with her art teacher. She's infatuated. Wonder if she'll ever copulate with anyone. People will fall in love with her: her wit, her hair, etc. She will probably be famous. As you may have guessed, I'm under the 'Brodie' influence. Went to see it last night at the Odeon with Morag. Horrid coming out of cinema. Everyone together in a big crowd. Everyone knows you've been to pictures. Embarrassing. That peculiar intangible sort of embarrassment.

They will destroy my cool room. It'll become the telly room!

Got a note from Trev today which he signed 'Yours as Ever'. He said if I didn't come to his house before 9.00 pm on Saturday he would go and get pissed and 'needless to say would be very pleased if I could see you'. Pedestal is being built again!

Saturday, 18th September

Mixed feeling meeting with Trev. I don't think he thinks much of my actual letters. He likes to get letters from me, he likes to think that I'm wanting to communicate with him, but he says he can't understand most of them. In other words, most of them are rubbish. Terrors and fears about 'A' levels haunt me incessantly; help me please, dear God.

Sunday, 19th September

Nancy does not seem to notice or need me nowadays. She slips further and further away from me every day. O Lord, give me someone! I'm fat and not doing enough work. Saw Thorpey and Caroline Ryder (with whom he went camping) today. He says he's in love with her. Who wouldn't be?

I'm sick of beautiful girls! Ruth MacIntyre's bra is at least three times too small for her — hideous mass of white flesh bulging out of a ghastly pink nylon bra.

I hope Nancy acknowledges my presence sooner or later, or her absence from me — not that it matters to her, but still.

Monday, 20th September

I think and hope that Tessa is my friend. We talked together a lot today. I felt as if I belonged to someone or something. I could tell Tessa anything without the feeling of possession of knowledge, i.e. no, I'll not tell her that, I'll keep it for myself, i.e. opinions or feelings about things. I try not to deny her anything. It's nice having someone to go home with, someone who waits for you, etc. I feel as if I have to work hard for it, though!

Wednesday, 22nd September

It seems ages since I've had any contact with Trev. Filled in my UCCA form. Cheap thrill!

Friday, 24th September

Trev wrote to me and I got it today. I think he loves me, which is bad. I feel undeservingly pedestalised. Nancy goes away to college on Tuesday. Bloody 'ell. She doesn't know how I feel about her leaving. At least I don't think she does. Won't be able to go to the station with her 'cos Dave'll be there probably, and it's he that counts most to her, so bloody 'ell. I don't want her to be away from me. Please don't let her forget me ever. But I fear I may fade into the backroom of her mind as just one of her sisters and nothing. What else am I, though?

Daniel's talking of buying a motorbike and going to Ghana to where Joanne is. I hope he and her last the year out. Our family seems always to have the problem of separation from loved ones—Daniel and Joanne, Morag and Miro, Nancy and Dave, me and Nancy.

Sunday, 26th September

She's going, she's bloody going. Dear God, please let her remember me and love me, or begin to love me.

Tuesday, 28th September

Nancy's gone and I realise I only know now what love is. Adrian Henri can go to hell! Oh God, it makes me realise how far away I was from the real meaning of love. As she was going I went upstairs and she came after me. She hugged me close and my tears came and I grabbed onto her, overwhelmed with happiness and sorrow by the thought that it mattered to her as much as it did to me. She cried for me, it mattered to her. O God, that moment. She really does care! But now she's gone. She cried and begged me to go and see her and write to her. She wanted me to! I realise only now that she is the only person whom I've ever loved or possibly ever will love. My love for her is so intense, so real. I doubt if after knowing such a powerful love I will ever love anybody quite as much. I really believe that.

> My ragges of heart can wish, like and adore
> But after one such love can love no more

> *John Donne*

I couldn't talk to anybody this morning at school, but I realised nobody cared, they probably thought: oh, she's in one of her sulks, she'll be all right in a bit. They wouldn't appreciate what it was all about. They would just think, oh well, it's only a sister. An early frost-morning bike ride helped a little, but not much. Tears almost poured on the bus, need to control, my eyes are swollen and my throat is lumpy and my heart is drained. This only serves to underline my belief that nothing ever lasts, ever. Me and Nancy are over, it will never be the same. She will become a visitor. We will never be as close, it has stopped, it has finished, and it hurts. I didn't think it would be so bad.

Wednesday, 29th September

Tessa refused to tell me who she was writing a letter to today. I know it's petty, but she's not really my friend or I'm not really her friend. It was significant that she wouldn't tell me, it hurt, 'cos I thought I had a friend. I'll have to look elsewhere.

Thursday, 30th September

Got a letter from Trev today. I am in no mood for writing a letter back. I hate coming home now. No reason to. I come home, eat my food and go out of the room. I've nothing to say to them. I don't want to talk to them. I feel like a lodger. I remember her tears every second.

October

Your Stars for October

Thunderous emotions can prevent you from thinking logically and can sometimes lead you to draw the wrong conclusions. If you're into soul-searching this month, don't allow gloom and despondency to cloud your judgement. If you're in need of company, join a drama club or some other such group, to satisfy that creative streak and make new friends at the same time. A new lipstick in a warm autumnal shade could help bring colour and zest to an otherwise dull and sagging social life.

Wednesday, 6th October

Nancy hasn't written. Maybe she didn't really care after all. Maybe she just cried because she was leaving home and not particularly me. Trev's coming up on Friday, don't want to see him really. Horrid arguments between Morag and Miro and Dad about Miro living here and living off Dad. New suite has arrived. Comfy. Dreamed of you, Nancy, rolling about on some hills with Tom from Woolies, and me telling you to stop it and to come up the hill with me but you wouldn't. You kept flirting and playing with Tom and he kept sitting on top of you and laughing and somehow you suffocated.

Thursday, 7th October

I realise, because of my love for Nancy, how much I do not love Trev. It must end. Before, I thought or I told myself that it wasn't a thing that could be 'finished' because it was a friendship like a girl/girl friendship or like a boy/boy or like a sister/brother friendship. That's what I made myself believe, but it's not. Because it was 'normal' (kisses) at the beginning it has had that tinge of boy/girl relationshipness ever since. I tried to make Trev something he wasn't. I give other people fantasy images of him and they fear him, in awe almost, which is a lie. What has made me realise how much our friendship is wrong is my love for Nancy—it must finish. Maybe I just can't be bothered to continue a relationship with him. But if I loved him enough I'd be bothered. He'll despise me after. He'll see through me. He'll wonder why on earth he ever sought after me in the first place. He'll laugh about me. He'll talk about me to his brother and sneer. His brother'll sneer.

I wish she'd write!

Friday, 8th October

I am home. I am alone. I'm sitting here. It's over. I'm thinking and feeling nothing, absolutely nothing — no sorrow, no nothing. Am I capable of feeling? I am. I know, because of Nancy. Trev cried and loved me, but I couldn't feel anything except relief. Why? Why can't I? He said all the time he'd wanted it to be more physical, he begged to let us still be friends. I think he won't write. I'm a neutral bitch, it hurt him God knows how deep. Christ, how could I? But here and now I don't feel anything. I don't wish, for instance, that we hadn't split. I don't wish anything except Nancy, please, dear God, let her love me.

Wednesday, 13th October

She has written!

Friday, 22nd October

I wait only now for half term and when I see Nancy. Thought of Nancy last night, having an old face. Growing old, seeing her wrinkled, horror. Go to Manchester on Tuesday for boots, posters. Buy on arrival in London flowers for Nancy.

November

YOUR STARS FOR NOVEMBER

Your time is precious these days and you therefore cannot afford to dabble in tawdry temporary relationships. Yours is an all-or-nothing policy, but try not to let your passions blind your common sense.

Monday, 1st November

> Have returned from London,
> tears have also returned,
> anguish and ripped hearts.
> My hopes, my one hope that
> Nancy needed me,
> has been murdered
> by a spear.
> Dave was there when I arrived
> and when I left.

The belief that has kept me going these past few weeks was that she needed me as a person who just happens to be a sister. But no. She needed a sister and I just happen to be a sister. She said that I had got to be her best friend now because she didn't have one any more. She needed a best friend, a sister. She didn't want me alone, for myself. The hardest thing to accept is that if she had just Dave and not me, she could survive, it would be enough, but if she had just me and not Dave it wouldn't be enough, there'd be a large gap, and it's no good me being happy if she isn't.

She says she loves me and that she loves Dave. Yeah, but he weighs more than I do. I can't stop myself but I am jealous of Dave. He said to me (about two people being on their own away from home, how they think in terms of 'we' all the time and they get really close), 'I don't think you can understand.'

My God!

He comes here after twelve months and tells me that I can't understand!

> I detest him.
> I want to rip his arm away from her body.

121

It's him who doesn't understand.
He possesses her
just because he's a boy.
Why! Why!
Oh, Christ,
I feel . . .

Does she just love me 'cos she sees how much I love her and how much it hurts me to leave her? Does her love for me stem from pity and guilt and politeness, like sending someone a card just because they sent you one?

Wednesday, 3rd November

Trip to see *Measure for Measure*. Pure rubbish. Michael Fisher bought me a drink. Tessa, Helen and me smoked on coach. Ruth MacIntyre's eyes fell out when I bought ten Embassy.

Saturday, 6th November

Trev came up to Rochdale last night. Stupid Trev.
    He thought that I wanted a physical relationship but becos of his shyness me and him didn't have one.
    Stupid, insensitive Trev.
    The number of times I've screamed internally, 'Nothing physical please.' He couldn't even sense that I didn't want a boy/girl relationship. He wanted to kiss me again last night. The stupid bugger.

Sunday, 7th November

Why has Nancy not written?

    It is sad

when that intense passion
cools
lukewarm
terrifying because it is
inevitable.

I fear that my missing her has become a mere feeling to be accepted and habitualised. It is frightening how my tears have dried up. Nothing ever lasts.

Monday, 8th November

Not much hope of a place at drama school, seeing as they don't like taking people straight from school. Mixed ideas, still unsettled about that ugly word 'career'. Tessa showed me photos of her and her boyfriend in London. She didn't show anyone else.

I've remembered about my visit to Nancy. On the Friday night me, Nancy and Dave went to a pub in Drury Lane called The White Hart. It was a pub with a small group playing live jazz. It was nice. We were all sat on a bench opposite an engaged couple. I was in the middle of Nancy and Dave, felt awkward. Couldn't talk. My tears came and poured and Nancy put her arm round me. I felt as if I was just visiting. I felt like a guest. Nancy came with me to wash my face. She said, 'You've got to be my best friend now 'cos I haven't got one.' Sharon Wilton has got married and apparently almost forgotten hers and Nancy's friendship, or else regards it as trivial. Nancy began to cry, but was she crying for me or because of the cessation of her and Sharon's friendship? I fear the latter was the cause.

Dave was good to me and Nancy after. He tried to make us happy and accepted me as a good person. He suggested us all getting drunk. I got merry on five gin and tonics. Dave said I'd got to come again to London before Christmas. It was so fantastic after that. But will she ever write? In London with Nancy and Dave, going down Portobello

Road on Saturday afternoon munching crisps—winter, dark, cold but happy.

Tuesday, 9th November

> To act
> to be
> to become other people in theatre
> one's own character
> must needs be
> neutral,
> type casting will occur if one has a set character of one's
>   own.
> But is total neutralisis
> Possible?

Many times Nancy and Dave's love for each other is overwhelming. The intensity and fantasticness of it overpowers me. It is like one of those immense and intangible things (e.g. time, God, etc.) in life that always make me cry 'cos they are so huge.

Wednesday, 10th November

Christmas will be awful. I'll just be one of the family that she's visiting. Morag has gone into hospital today. What is the Mass for? Why do I go? Nancy is Dave's girl first and my friend second. If I stopped being her friend she wouldn't break down. If Dave stopped being her boyfriend she'd break down completely. Conclusion: nothing now. I'm not really anything to Nancy, I am just by the wayside. I thought I meant much more to her. I made too much of me and Nancy's friendship. I built it up in my mind and in her absence out of proportion, out of loneliness.

Friday, 12th November

Went to Gerard Bailey's party. Louis Frazer. Physical! We danced and sweated together till 2 in the morning. So dry for a year almost shrivelled. He's a ladies' man. He hates men, he says, and he needs women. He's already done his 'A' levels: two As and a B. I believe him. He lives up Syke Pond in the bungalows. Dope smoker, but he says he's off acid himself.

All Trev's friends were there.

Saturday, 13th November

Met Louis in the Robin Hood. We talked. Thank God. Feared that it might have been too physical and talk would not have come. But it was good. It was almost a combination. His girlfriend Suzy is in Blackburn and he goes out with me. Somehow feel proud. He doesn't care much for her but she sleeps with him so I suppose it goes okay. It's going on longer than I ever imagined. He'll get bored. Old dusky blue suede jacket, nice hair, body. Hate saying the name Louis, sounds so flash and groovy. He's going to Blackburn on Wednesday. He talked about Suzy.

'She's not particularly good in bed,' he said. 'You know what Suzy calls me? Loulou. Hiya, Loulou, that's what she writes in letters. Fuckin' 'ell.'

He told me of his dreams where he tried to merge me and Suzy into one. She is not enough. He wants us both. But he'll probably settle for half. He said she woke him up with a phone call. He said as soon as he woke up he knew he had to phone me. He said, 'Suzy's always a long time on the phone. It really bugs me, that.' He's only been going out with her since August. She's probably tremendously sexy and beautiful.

He's not worth wasting my 'A' level chances for. The charmer. He regards going to bed as a matter of course. I asked him whether he'd been to bed with all the girls he'd been out with recently. He said yes. I asked him, were they easy? He couldn't understand. He said there was no question of it being either easy or difficult to 'get them into bed'. It just happened because they wanted to and so did he at the time. Oh, crikey!

Tuesday, 16th November

Two letters from Trev. One hard and accusing, calling me a cheap bitch. I am no nun. I thought I could be. I pretended. The second was don't carish. 'Couldn't give a fuck. Forget it.' I must write.

Wednesday, 17th November

It is Wednesday and Louis has gone to Blackburn with the promise that he'll see me as soon as he gets back. He said, 'It can't be permanent with you because you've got University, but Suzy isn't going to University, so . . .'
   Was sick in the Robin Hood toilets last night. He was worried and it was nice being with him. He held my arm. It'll finish as soon as an opportunity for us going to bed arises and I refuse. He thinks I'm not a virgin. He thinks my profile is fantastic. Big deal. And I said to him and he said to me bla bla bla bla. Good grief, I am getting girly.

Thursday, 18th November

Horrific dreams last night. Me and Louis were left in the house on our own and he took it for granted that we'd go to bed. I ran and ran, trying to get to Karen's house in Churchill Street. Woke up breathless. Went back to sleep and dreamed that I was in bed with Louis and that we got up the next morning and Mum and Dad watched us getting dressed. Could feel his flesh on top of mine. Terror. He came to our house again later that day and I asked him whether we'd had it last night and he said, 'Oh yes, we had it all right, baby, we had it.' God, it was horrific. Thank God it was only a dream.

Saturday, 20th November

Sat in the Castle pub with Louis and realised that he is the original big-head, me me bloody me all the time. Incredible and intolerable. I insulted his masculinity by not going to bed with him. 'I've never failed yet'—fuckin' 'ell! I don't and didn't like him as a person. It was all physical. He gave me a day-to-day account of his stay in Blackburn. He is self-centred, egocentric—bed was the beginning and the end of it all. God, it sounds so corny, but that is all he wanted. If I saw Louis in town anytime I would have nothing to say to him at all. Nothing. I'm glad it's over but fear the consequences: I'm not seeing him again therefore he could be nasty, he could talk and spread rumours. Louis had an obsession about pure white skin. Who cares?

Sunday, 21st November

Felt annoyed last night yet curiously free and liberated this morning. I live again in singularity. I have no need of plurals.

Monday, 22nd November

Sat in Latin today thinking about going to Italy with Trev. Hope we go. Hope he writes. I realise Louis was merely a person to fill in the gap left by Nancy. Superficial compensation. Maybe I should be glad and grateful for having known such a love as mine for her.

Saturday, 27th November

On an 'A' level course personal problems are not allowed.
Letters between me and Nancy, tears, puffed eyes.

December

YOUR STARS FOR DECEMBER

You could be in for a tough time this month if you allow disappointments at home, at work or in love to get you down. Remember, as one door closes another usually opens. Tantrums will get you nowhere. Friends and family will go out of their way to let you know how much they love you, but ultimately it's up to you whether or not you listen and learn.

Sunday, 5th December

Went to Manchester University Theatre last night on my own to listen to some poetry readings. There was an interval. I didn't go out for coffee, I stayed in my seat and then I looked up and Nancy was standing there. I thought it was a hallucination. Couldn't believe it. Tears and hugs. She had come to see me! I wrote her a letter and she'd received it Saturday morning. She was crying and Dave read it and said, 'Tell her I love her too.' She started to write back to me but decided it was stupid and so they hitched up here. Dad drove her to the University Theatre and there she was. God! Intense happiness. She had done it for me. She had hitched up just to see me. She did it to show me that me and her mattered. Dad gave me a knowing smile/beaming.

Thursday, 9th December

Letters between Nancy and I have cooled down — casual, happy, chatty letters. It is sad.

Friday, 10th December

I'm feeling bad. Why does Nancy have it so good? I feel so domesticated, so fat, so stay-at-homish, so secondary and so sheepish when I'm with her. And yet I love her. But my love for her is useless. Whatever happens me and her will lead separate lives. Dave is her life and I'm an accessory. A necessary accessory? I think not.

Monday, 13th December

Nancy is going to marry Dave next summer. This will no longer be her bedroom. She will no longer tell me everything. She will become a wife who tells everything to her husband. I will become an acquaintance who is privileged by snippets of gossip, etc., and nothing more. Why must it be me she leaves and not Dave if she says she loves me? She cannot. Just because I'm a bloody girl and the pattern of life is that we leave our friends of the same sex and go and live with our husbands, that the pattern may subsist.

I am being used. All this time I've been used by her. She who told me she loved me. She used me. I was there for her to talk to in the intervals when she was waiting for Dave, or to hear all when she came back from seeing Dave. All her real time was spent with him. Now I know where I stand, as they say. Why must she get married next summer? Why? She couldn't give a fuck what happens to me next year. The months I've prayed, the nights I've cried and prayed that Nancy and Dave get back together again. The tears I cried when they split up. Oh, everything must be done to make sure that Nancy and Dave's relationship is preserved. Why is it so bloody important? They'll probably get married in Switzerland. Oh, Nancy and Dave's wedding cannot be ordinary. I suppose I'd better be grateful for a piece of wedding cake — that's if they can spare it. Okay, I'm fucked up with jealousy. I'm going to be in a right good frame of mind for doing my 'A' levels now, aren't I!

Tuesday, 14th December

I blame her. I blame her for allowing me to get like her, to get to love her, for pouring myself out in front of her, for letting me strip myself naked in front of her, saying she loves me. And then she gets up and walks away. What the bloody hell does she expect me to do? Sit here and let her go? Would she expect Dave to sit there and let her go? I can see now I had no pride where Nancy was concerned. We have been living a lie. We suppress anger and feelings. We don't say things because it would maybe hurt the other. I once believed that my relationship with Nancy was the best I'd ever known or ever would know. It was open, honest and so good it made me shake with happiness. But then things started to curdle, things began to go sour. We let things go unsaid. We didn't say as much. I was jealous and never said. We drifted apart and now we're on opposite sides of the river.

Wednesday, 15th December

My days contain too many thoughts to ever contain them in
  this book.
My days are leaking with tears.
She
She has done this to me.

Saturday, 18th December

Went out with Nancy and Dave in Rochdale last night. Maybe I'm ungrateful, but I felt as if they'd asked me to come out with them out of pity—not exactly pity, but charity, something like that. It was pretty obvious that they'd rather be on their own. Just once in a while. Thank you very much, that leaves me in again on Saturday night. It's at night I feel most depressed. No, not depressed, just miserable and hopeless. Must I at last accept that it will always be like this concerning Nancy? Yes. Lord, lift me out of my present state for my exams. Let me pretend I'm so happy. So bloody happy.

Me being full of romantic ideas, thanks to Adrian Henri and all that lot, I wish I could have been a teenager going out with someone and meeting him after school in my uniform. I've had my bloody chance! My time is up. There's none left.

Epilogue

It is now the 1980s
ten years after . . .

Dear Sir,

I am writing to apply for a place in your company. As you can see from the enclosed photograph, I'm a pleasant enough girl but I have had my problems.

My C.V. is as follows: I was born in the 'fifties so I go a bundle on men who know how to rock and roll, I went to RADA where I walked off with every prize and medal that was going, so I'm a bit of a big-head. The parts I've played and excelled at in the past are: Northern intellectual blue stocking, over-rated poet and paramour *extraordinaire*. My skills include the ability to give as good as I get, proficiency in pudding making and a newly acquired insight into the meaning of classical love poetry. If you think you can make use of me and my skills in your company I should be more than willing to attend for audition.

P.S. I can't sing and I've got two left feet, but catch me when I'm happy and it's a different story.

Yours in earnest.